"The book is truly a 'Bible' of the field....
By far the best book on flight attendants I've ever seen."
— *Career Opportunities News*

"The **definitive guide** to entering and prospering in this specialized profession. If you aspire to a flight attendant career, then begin by reading the *Flight Attendant Job Finder & Career Guide.*" — *Midwest Book Review*

"**Must reading** for anyone contemplating a flight attendant career.... **very thorough** overview about what a flight attendant's life is all about....

"While obviously enthusiastic, Kirkwood does not put a sugar coating on his profession, but rather presents the facts in an **effective** manner, and lets the reader decide. It's a **refreshing** approach." — *Airways*

"Gathers **information not found in a single location elsewhere**." — *Milwaukee Journal*

The *Flight Attendant Job Finder & Career Guide* provides you with all the insider information, strategies, requirements, and details you need to be among that elite ten percent of flight attendant applicants who get hired.

It gets you to airlines that are actually hiring today: the lesser-known regional airlines, charters, and corporate flyers.

And it delivers to you the **most thorough** and **up-to-date** directory of airlines so you can intelligently decide which airlines you want to work for — a crucial decision because the seniority system strongly discourages changing airlines at any time during your flight attendant career!

Other career books from Planning/Communications:

- ✗ *International Job Finder: Where the Jobs are Worldwide*
- ✗ *How to Get a Job In Europe*
- ✗ *Government Job Finder*
- ✗ *Nonprofits Job Finder*
- ✗ *Education Job Finder*
- ✗ *Professional's Job Finder*
- ✗ *From Making a Profit to Making a Difference:*
  How to Launch Your New Career in Nonprofits

Visit http://jobfindersonline.com
for excerpts from all the books
Planning/Communications publishes
as well as free updates and news
about forthcoming books.

77TH ANNIVERSARY EDITION

Flight Attendant JOB FINDER & CAREER GUIDE

Tim Kirkwood

PLANNING/COMMUNICATIONS

River Forest, Illinois

For quantity discounts and permissions, contact the publisher:

Planning/Communications

7215 Oak Avenue, River Forest, Illinois 60305; phone: 708/366–5200
Websites: http://planningcommunications.com
http://jobfindersonline.com
email: info@planningcommunications.com

Distribution to bookstores:
Contact Planning/Communications for information.

Cover design by Salvatore Concialdi
Interior design by Rick Barry

Produced using Corel Ventura 8.
Photograph on page 64 used by permission of the
Corel Corporation. All rights reserved.

Disclaimer of All Warranties and Liabilities

While every effort has been taken to assure the accuracy and timeliness of the information contained in this book, the author and publisher make no warranties, either expressed or implied, with respect to the information contained herein. The author and publisher shall not be liable for any incidental or consequential damages in connection with, or arising out of, the use of materials in this book.

Publisher's Cataloging–in–Publication Data
(Provided by Quality Books, Inc.)

Kirkwood, Tim, 1953 –

Flight attendant job finder & career guide / Tim Kirkwood
— 77th anniversary ed.

p. cm.
Includes bibliographical references
Preassigned LCCN: 2002105556
ISBN: 1–884587–14–3 (pbk.)

1. Flight attendants—Vocational guidance. 2. Job hunting.
I. Title. II Title: Flight attendant job finder and career guide

HD8039.A43K57 2003   387.7'42'02373
                                       QBI98–1392

Table of Contents

✈ DEDICATION

In this, the 77th anniversary of the first airplane flight with flight attendants, the *Flight Attendant Job Finder & Career Guide* is dedicated to all those in the airline industry who have fought so long and so hard to put the "pro" in "professional."

✈ ACKNOWLEDGMENTS

I would like to thank the people who made this book possible. Special thanks go to the professionals at the In–Flight and Human Resources departments of the airlines for their invaluable assistance, and to the flight attendants who contributed their ideas and views.

Special thanks go to Helen McLaughlin for her wonderful book *Footsteps in the Sky* and her remarkable assistance, to Vicky Morris Young's help with the historic aspects of this career, and to Georgia Panter–Nielson for all the background information she supplied for the chapter on flight attendant unions. I am indebted to Susan Friedenberg for her tireless assistance with the chapter on corporate flight attendants, and for allowing me to learn from and use her copyrighted training materials.

And heartfelt gratitude to my publisher, Daniel Lauber, for his continued support and dedication to keeping my dream alive.

— Tim Kirkwood

✈ USING THIS GUIDE

Both the flight attendant profession and its job application process are like no other. The *Flight Attendant Job Finder & Career Guide* seeks to escort you through the complex and often perplexing process of getting hired as a flight attendant by the airline of your choice. You would be very prudent to read this guide from the beginning before you examine the airline listings in Chapter 25. You will need to fully understand the nature of the job and career, as well as the application and interviewing process, before you start selecting the airlines for which you want to work.

By using this guide, you will be able to concentrate on the airlines that meet your requirements or preferences for both your job and your career. For the airlines to which you apply, this book helps bring to the interviewing process candidates for employment who are knowledgeable and well-prepared for the position.

Every effort has gone into structuring this book to make it easy to find the information you seek. To avoid needlessly killing more trees, we have not included an index.

The information contained in this guide has been gathered from flight attendants and the Human Resources and In-Flight Personnel departments of the airlines described in Chapter 25. The author has done everything possible to ensure its accuracy and timeliness. But information changes rapidly in the airline industry. Be sure to periodically obtain the latest free update to this book as explained on page 167. This guide will help your efforts to launch or advance your flight attendant career. But like all other career books, it cannot guarantee you will get hired. It does, however, give you all the information and tools you need to find job openings for flight attendants and successfully navigate the unusual hiring process for this unique job.

✈ INTRODUCTION

You've seen them in the movies: flying to exotic and faraway places, spending luxurious days in Paris and Rome, indulging the every whim of their wealthy (and single!) first–class passengers before they jet back to their smartly furnished apartments in Midtown Manhattan. The passengers on their flights are all happy, calm, and very sophisticated — and they always have plenty of time to chat with each and every passenger. The airplanes that carry them are spacious and comfortable, with aisles so wide you could drive a truck down them. And they all look like models from the pages of *Vogue* and *GQ*. How could you not want to be a flight attendant?

Real life is much different than the movies — a fact you must accept before you even consider starting the challenging application process to become a flight attendant. While the above scenario may have been somewhat true during the height of the industry in the sixties and seventies, airline deregulation has vastly altered the industry. Prior to deregulation, the federal government set airline fares and routes, which made the system fair for all airlines, regardless of size. The abolition of those regulations in 1978 freed airlines to set fares and routes at whatever the market would bear. In addition, the events of September 11, 2001, will be seen as the turning point of a new phase of the airline industry — the results of which still await us. More than ever before, "survival of the fittest" and "maximizing profits" are the airline industry's mantras. Dollars and cents control most management decisions, which has led airlines to cut costs wherever they can.

"Maximizing productive crew utilization" has become the standards in the airline industry. This approach translates into more work and longer hours for the same or even lower wages. The *Flight Attendant Job Finder & Career Guide* escorts you through the real world that daily greets every flight attendant. It helps you answer the questions, "Am I right for this career, and is this career right for me?"

✈ Chapter 1
HISTORY OF FLIGHT ATTENDANTS

Back in the 1920s and 1930s, Postmasters General Brown and Farley established the network of U.S. airways after Congress assigned them the power to consolidate air mail routes in the "best interest" of the American public. At first, only mail was flown, but gradually passenger traffic started to build. In 1922, Daimler Airways of Britain did something remarkable: It hired the world's first airplane stewards. Undoubtedly hired because of their small stature, cabin boys reportedly did not serve any refreshments but offered passengers general assistance and reassurance.

"Couriers" — that's what the first flight attendants were called in the United States. Their ranks included the young sons of the steamship, railroad, and industrial magnates who financed the airlines. In 1926, Stout Air Services of Detroit became the first U.S. airline to employ male aerial couriers, working on Ford Tri–Motor planes between Detroit and Grand Rapids, Michigan. Stout became part of the United Airlines conglomerate in 1929. Then Western (1928), and Pan Am (1929) were the first U.S. carriers to employ stewards to serve food. Pan American steward Joey Carrera recalls how the crew would lug along several days worth of food because nothing edible could be found at their stopover points. In the early flying boats, the so-called galley was in the tail of the plane, and could be reached only by crawling on hands and knees through a low, narrow passageway. Returning to the passenger cabin while balancing food and drink took genuine skill. Stewards also worked on the ten-passenger Fokkers in the Caribbean as gamblers traveled between Key West, Florida, and Havana, Cuba.

During the early days of commercial aviation, a pilot or first officer would often leave the cockpit to serve as a cabin attendant — helping serve the passengers in addition to helping fly the planes. But this splitting of duties proved inefficient, so airlines began to consider other options.

Boeing Air Transport (BAT), a forerunner of United Air Lines, was the first airline to hire women. Registered nurse Ellen Church convinced Steven A. Stimpson, then District Traffic Manager for BAT, to consider using women as flight attendants. BAT's executives allowed Mr. Stimpson to conduct a three–month trial of women flight attendants, hiring Ms.

> In addition to meal service, stewardesses were responsible for winding the clock and altimeters in the cabin and ensuring that the wicker passenger seats were securely bolted to the aircraft floor.

Church as Chief Stewardess supervising seven other nurses. On May 15, 1930, the world's "Original Eight" stewardesses flew for the first time.

Airline executives believed the presence of a female attendant on board would reassure passengers of the increasing safety of air travel. They thought it would be difficult for potential travelers to admit their fear of flying when young women were part of the in-flight crew. They also believed that women would cater to their predominately male passengers. They were right on target. By the end of the three-month trial, passenger bookings were steadily increasing and male passengers were arranging to fly on specific flights with their favorite stewardess. Not everyone was enthusiastic about the idea of female attendants, though. Pilots claimed they were too busy flying to have to look after "helpless" female crew members.

Flying on Boeing 80s and 80-As, stewardesses would serve their ten passengers a cold meal, usually fried chicken, apples, and sandwiches, which they would pick up at the hanger before passengers boarded the plane. On flights out of Chicago, the famous Palmer House Hotel catered the food. In 1931, Eastern Air Transport hostesses served passengers in a hanger at Richmond, Virginia. On Curtiss-Wright Condor aircraft (which had no galleys) hostesses served their 18 passengers coffee, tea, Coca-Cola, biscuits, and coffeecake from a picnic hamper. United used fine bone china until turbulence rendered that practice economically unsound. Coffee was served from thermos bottles.

In addition to meal service, stewardesses were also responsible for winding clocks and altimeters in the cabin, swatting flies, and ensuring that the wicker passenger seats were securely bolted to the aircraft floor with the wrench they carried as part of their crew baggage. They were also required to advise passengers not to throw lighted

cigars and cigarettes out aircraft windows while flying over populated areas and to make sure that passengers used the lavatory door rather than the exit door when in flight! Harriet Fry Iden, one of the "Original Eight" recalls, "Our lavatory was very nice with hot and cold water, but the toilet was a can set in a ring and a hole cut in the floor, so when one opened the toilet seat, behold, open air toilet!"

Stewardesses had to be between 5 feet, 2 inches and 5 feet, 5 inches, well–proportioned, without glasses and with good teeth. Some airlines even included calf, ankle and thigh measurements in their hiring requirements. They wore dresses, hats gloves and high heels! At this time, stewardesses earned $110 (Eastern) to $125 (Boeing Air Transport) per month. Raises were unheard of during the Great Depression. At the beginning of 1933, there were only 38 stewardess in the United States. Twenty–six worked for United, on Boeing aircraft; the other 12 worked for Eastern on Curtiss–Wright Condors. On May 3, 1933, American Air Ways, predecessor of American Airlines, hired its first four hostesses and a week later, hired two more registered nurses. By the time Trans–Canada Air Lines (later renamed Air Canada) was created in April 1937, the stewardess concept was firmly in place.

In the beginning, airlines preferred to hire only registered nurses, not just for their medical experience but also because it was believed that nurses' disciplined life would transfer well to the rigors of airline travel. During World War II, the requirement was dropped because nurses were needed in the war effort, and the airlines hired only men to work on the Civil Reserve Air Fleet (CRAF) flights, which opened the job market for women on non–military commercial flights.

It is crucial that you study the listings in Chapter 25 to make the most informed choice when selecting a carrier.

The stewardess career gradually evolved from something a woman performed for an average of two years before she married into a long–term career for women and men until retirement age. This has largely been a result of better wage and benefits packages secured by unions on behalf of various flight attendant work forces. In the "old days," stewardesses were required to quit when they got married or became pregnant.

Airlines initially hired only young women as flight attendants. Some airlines preferred that they retire or transfer to a ground job by their mid–30s! These unjustifiable policies were rendered illegal by the Civil Rights Act of 1964, Equal Employment Opportunity Commission guidelines, and numerous discrimination lawsuits. Today, airlines cannot refuse to hire somebody due to race, religion, national origin, age, disability unrelated to performing a specific job, marital status, or gender. As more men entered the profession, the job title changed from "stewardess or steward" to the current moniker of "flight attendant." While some countries continue to use the job titles "steward and stewardess" or even "host and

The "Original Eight" stewardesses. Ellen Church is in the upper left.
Photo courtesy of United Air Lines. Used by permission.

hostess," the trend is to use the gender–free "flight attendant" or "cabin crew" sobriquets. Today the average age of flight attendants ranges from the late 20s to mid–30s. Average seniority is ten years with a very low attrition rate. About half are married, while the rest include singles, divorcees, surviving spouses, parents, and even grandparents!

Before 1978, the Federal Government set airfares. All airlines charged the same ticket price to the same destination. So, if three different airlines flew the New York to Los Angeles route, the ticket price was the same on all three carriers. To entice you to choose them over the others, airlines offered amenities. Consequently, food service was much better than exists today, with steak a regular entrée on the menu. In–flight movies, music, and even a piano bar on jumbo jets were offered to attract your business. During this period, flight attendants were considered part of the package as well. Airlines chose young, slender and pretty women, and then dressed them in mini–skirts or hot pants. Airline advertising promoted this sexuality with slogans such as "We really move our tail for you," or "I'm Sally...fly me!"

The Airline Deregulation Act of 1978 took the power to set fares away from the government, and gave it to the airlines themselves, opening the door to corporate greed. The fare wars that followed led airlines to reduce or abandon many amenities. Gone were the elaborate food services and piano bar. Flight attendant staffing was also reduced on each flight while passenger seats were added.

To save additional money, airlines attempted to roll salaries back to 1970 levels. Bargaining power was weakened, and over half the airlines that existed before deregulations went bankrupt, merged, or were forced out of business. Out of all the new start–up airlines that grew out of deregulation, only America West is still in business today.

Unfortunately, since the terrorist attacks of September 11, 2001, the outlook for flight attendants in the new millennium is uncertain as more airlines file for protection under Chapter 11 bankruptcy or merge with stronger carriers. If you are considering serving as a flight attendant as a long–term career, it is crucial that you study the listings in this guide to make the most informed choice possible when selection a carrier for which to work.

You would be prudent to research the history and prospects of the airlines you are considering. Sources for this information include business newspapers and magazines, which you can find at your local library. In addition, the World Wide Web, or Internet can provide you with good information on individual airlines, simply by visiting their websites. The Airline Listings that begin on page 81 include the web addresses for each airline. Nearly every website has an "Our Company" or "History" section that will give you additional background on the airline, its formation, and corporate personnel. Most will also have an "Employment" or "Careers" section that may furnish more information on hiring requirements, or upcoming open house interview sessions. Knowing an airline's history and its current policies can be invaluable when you are interviewed as is explained in Chapter 14 beginning on page 42.

Some of the best and most accessible sources can be flight attendants who work for your preferred airline. Spend a day at your local airport interviewing flight attendants while they're waiting for their flights. Ask them about working conditions, pay rates, management attitude, job security, and airline policies. They can tell you which of their domiciles are the most junior, or the most senior — see page 56 for details. Show them your copy of the *Flight Attendant Job Finder & Career Guide* and ask them any questions you might have about their airline's listing.

For further reading on the subject of flight attendant history, there is no better book than Helen McLaughlin's *Footsteps in the Sky,* noted in the "Additional References" starting on page 168. Her collection of first–person accounts from the first stewardesses to present–day flight attendants can give you a better insight and awareness of the career path you have chosen.

✈ **Chapter 2**
CHANGES SEPTEMBER 11 HATH WROUGHT

There's no question that the deadly terrorist attacks on September 11, 2001, will affect the role of flight attendants and their training for many years to come.

These attacks made aviation history. All commercial aircraft were grounded as a security precaution within three hours of the three planes crashing into the World Trade Towers and the Pentagon. This grounding — the first of its kind since the dawn of aviation — may have saved countless lives by preventing additional attacks. Twenty-six flight attendants died in those attacks that forever changed the way airlines deal with security. What didn't change was the way airlines deal with passenger and crew safety.

Prior to September 11, airline crews were trained to keep the hijackers and passengers calm. They were trained to do as the hijackers demanded. The goal was to get the aircraft on the ground, and let professionally trained law–enforcement personnel work on disarming the hijackers. Flight attendants cooperated with the hijackers in those days and would actually quell any attempts by the passengers to fight back. In some cases, negotiations to release the passengers and crew took weeks.

September 11 changed all that because those hijackers didn't intend to land the aircraft. They didn't want to be talked out of it. They wanted to use the airplanes as flying missiles, and they succeeded all too well. Once that became evident to the passengers and crew on the fourth hijacked flight, they fought back, and probably saved hundreds of lives when their plane crashed in the Pennsylvania countryside instead of the White House or other target. This was a radical departure from the training the flight attendants had received, and it proved that new thinking was required.

These tragic events have led to changes in the training the entire crew receives. The cockpit door is now barred from outside entry, with a complex set of entry codes required to even deliver meals to the pilots. Flight attendants are now the last remaining line of defense for the passengers and the cockpit crew. For this reason, many airlines now offer flight attendants classes in self–defense, tailored to an aviation environment. The exact tactics and training to thwart a threat to your flight are very confidential to avoid giving potential terrorists any advantage. Airline crew members are not allowed to discuss this security training and tactics with anyone outside their airline.

But any passenger since September 11 cannot help but notice that flight attendants are more serious and vigilant than ever before. An attendant will block passenger access to an open cockpit door with his body and food cart. If too many passengers stand near the lavatory, the attendant will ask some to sit down.

Sky Marshals on random flights assist in the event of a threat to the crew. They fly incognito so terrorists cannot single them out. Screening methods are being tightened and implemented on a weekly basis — all in an effort to remove the element of danger from air travel and your career.

The job of being a flight attendant has changed as a result of September 11. Airline crews are much more alert to, and airlines have a lot less tolerance for, problem or suspicious passengers. Passenger "air rage" is no longer tolerated, and the legal system backs this up with stiff fines and jail time for offenders. Passengers and pilots once again accord flight attendants the respect they have always deserved. More attention is paid to their observations and insights. As a working professional, you will be trained to deal with a variety of different in–flight situations and scenarios. Studies have consistently shown that well–trained crews that constantly review and reinforce the tactics learned are able to perform in an emergency without hesitation. In most cases, it has been the leadership of the flight attendants that has enabled passengers and even fellow crew members to survive an aviation incident. As a flight attendant, you must remain vigilant of suspicious behavior, and always protect the integrity of your uniform, ID card, and the cohesiveness of your crew.

So, how dangerous is a career as an airline flight attendant? Statistically, you have a far greater chance of being struck by lightening than dying in an airplane crash. In fact, you should be more terrified of crossing your local intersection or driving your car than of boarding an aircraft. Airplane incidents and crashes simply garner more attention from the news media than more mundane events such as car crashes or pedestrian hit–and–runs.

Even after September 11, few flight attendants quit their jobs to pursue a "safer" career.

Even after the terrorist attacks of September 11, few flight attendants quit their jobs to pursue a "safer" career. Some may have taken some time off to reflect, but the vast majority continued to report for their flights and do their part to return the industry back to normal. If anything, flight attendants are more dedicated than ever to keeping the actions of a select few from to disrupting their industry again. And odds are, with our heightened awareness and stricter security, there will never be another successful terrorist attempt against aviation.

Even so, the aviation industry studies each incident, and implements changes based on its findings to prevent a similar event in the future. By applying these changes, each year it becomes safer and safer to fly. In your annual safety training review, you will discuss the incidents of the previous year and learn new ways to incorporate additional safety and security measures into your daily work regime.

Despite over 77 years of passenger travel, the relationship between the airlines and passengers is very fragile. If passengers think flying is unsafe, they will flock to other means of transportation, and the airlines would quickly go out of business. For this reason, airlines are highly motivated and dedicated to providing all passengers with the highest possible level of safety. If this level of safety were to be applied to all aspects of our lives, our world would be a much safer place.

Chapter 3

FLIGHT ATTENDANT UNIONS

Flight attendant unions have been instrumental in securing fairness in labor contracts for their members.

Ada Brown, a United Airlines stewardess, formed the first flight attendant union (the Air Line Stewardesses Association) in 1945 to combat inequality in the workplace. Today seven flight attendant unions are headquartered in the U.S. and Canada: Association of Professional Flight Attendants (APFA), Transport Workers Union (TWU), Association of Flight Attendants (AFA), Canadian Airline Flight Attendants Association (CAFAA), International Brotherhood of Teamsters (IBT), Paper and Allied Chemical Engineers (PACE), and International Association of Machinists and Aerospace Workers (IAM).

The **Association of Professional Flight Attendants**, the largest independent aviation union in the world, represents 20,000 flight attendants at American Airlines alone. APFA is headquartered in Euless, Texas, close to the Dallas–Fort Worth International Airport. Flight attendants at American Airlines negotiated their first contract in 1947 as the Airline Stewards and Stewardesses Association (ALSSA). In 1961, they became a part of the Transport Workers Union (TWU), and formed an independent local union within TWU in 1974. In 1977 they founded APFA as an independent union.

The **Transport Workers Union** chartered a new local in Miami, Florida, just 11 years after its birth in 1934. When a few hundred workers from the Pan American overhaul base in Miami approached TWU to establish an organization, airline employees gained the opportunity to bargain effectively for better wages, work hours, and working conditions. Later, union members voted to certify TWU as the bargaining agent for the ground and flight service personnel at Pan

American Airways. Today, TWU represents nearly 50,000 workers.

The **Association of Flight Attendants** is the collective bargaining agent for 50,000 flight attendants on 26 air carriers. The union that became AFA was founded in 1945 and later became a part of the Air Line Pilots Association. In 1973, the flight attendant leadership voted to make AFA autonomous from ALPA, which was first certified in 1975. Chartered by the American Federation of Labor–Congress of Industrial Organizations (AFL–CIO) in February 1984, AFA is the largest flight attendant union in the world.

The **International Association of Machinists** was formed way back in 1888. It added flight attendants at Continental Airlines to its ranks in 1991 and now represents 12,000 flight attendants at Continental, Continental Express, and Continental Micronesia.

The **Canadian Airline Flight Attendants Association** became the Airline Division of the Canadian Union of Public Employees (CUPE) in November 1986. CUPE represents 10,000 flight attendants at five Canadian airlines.

The **Paper & Allied Chemical Engineer** union (PACE) resulted from the merger of UPIU and OCAW. Since the 1980s, the UPIU and the OCAW had worked together to provide a progressive voice inside the AFL-CIO and internationally. Both unions had been leaders in the effort to internationalize their own members' campaigns and to render assistance to unions abroad. On January 4, 1999, the two unions came together in simultaneous conventions, and approved the merger by voice vote. PACE now represents 147 flight attendants at Pinnacle Airlines.

The **International Brotherhood of Teamsters** (IBT) represents more than 1.4 million active members employed in a wide range of industries in the United States, Canada, and Puerto Rico. The IBT negotiated the freight industry's first national agreement in 1964 and began its efforts to unionize the airline industry in 1966 with employees of Western Airlines. The only union that represents every craft of workers in the airline industry, the Teamsters cover 18,000 flight attendants at 50 airlines.

> **The goal of every flight attendant union is to win reasonable pay and favorable working conditions through contract negotiations.**

Eastern Airlines stewards photograph reprinted by permission of Helen McLaughlin. Copyright 1994. All rights reserved.

If a union represents the flight attendants at the carrier you wish to work for, you are required to join that union once you are hired. Monthly union dues are either automatically deducted from your paycheck or you pay them every month.

All flight attendants at an airline belong to the same union. There are a few airlines where flight attendants do not have the benefit of a union. Flight attendant unions differ in size and name, but their purpose and structure are relatively similar. The goal of every flight attendant union is to negotiate contracts that maximize pay and working conditions. Unions also strive for better insurance, medical, and retirement benefits as well as pass privileges to fly on your employer airline for only a small service charge. Other negotiable items include scheduling restrictions and legalities, and improvements in hotel accommodations. The main objective is always to improve overall working conditions and strengthen the flight attendant's status as a professional. At the same time, unions have battled against gender, age and race discrimination, wrongful discipline or discharge, and unfair labor practices.

For an excellent account of the formation of the first flight attendant union, see the book *From Sky Girl To Flight Attendant* by Georgia Panter–Nielsen listed under "Additional References" beginning on page 168.

✈ Chapter 4
MINIMUM REQUIREMENTS FOR THE JOB

Airline officials usually say they are looking to hire flight attendants with a pleasant personality who work well with people. While this is generally true, there are additional criteria that can help you get hired. The more education, work experience, and skills that you bring to the interview, the better your chances of standing out from the crowd of applicants who also think they are perfect for the job.

There are times on the job when flight attendants must call upon every personal resource available to get them through difficult situations. You must learn how to interact with people from around the world, respecting individual customs and cultures. Your passengers may have a fear of flying, residual anger from a bad day at work, or a general disorientation due to the unfamiliar surroundings of an aircraft. The only way to learn how to deal with the public is to work with people. This is why airlines put so much emphasis on previous work experience that involves public contact.

Being a flight attendant is a job that offers the opportunity to meet and relate with people from all walks of life. As a flight attendant, you are given an education that can't be found in any book. You will become more aware of current events, not only because of the people you meet, but because you are often in the very place where news is happening. You may even find yourself a part of news in the making by working on Papal charters, inaugural flights, diplomatic shuttles, or press tours.

The absolute minimum requirements you must meet to qualify to be hired as a flight attendant include:

✂ **General:** U.S. airlines require a social security card. You will also need to submit to a background check of your previous ten years of education and employment, as well as fingerprinting.

The more job and personal skills you bring to an interview, the better your chances of standing out from the crowd.

✈ **Age:** The minimum age ranges from 18 to 21 years. There is no maximum age. Today, airlines are actively recruiting applicants in their 30s, 40s and 50s.

✈ **Height:** The usual range is five feet, two inches to six feet tall. Some airlines hire individuals as short as five feet, while others will hire people as tall as six feet, two inches.

✈ **Weight:** All airlines look for applicants whose weight is in proportion to their height, and avoid the strict height/weight charts that were used in the 1970s and 1980s. Some airlines require that your reach exceed a minimum length — 75 inches is the average

✈ **Vision:** Must be 20/20 or correctable to 20/20. All airlines allow flight attendants to wear glasses or contact lenses. Glasses worn in–flight must be conservative in style. All airlines accept applicants who have had laser surgery to correct their vision.

✈ **Health:** Candidates must be in excellent physical condition and able to pass a thorough physical examination as well as a drug test conducted by the company physician prior to employment. Random drug and alcohol tests will be administered throughout your airline career in accord with federal guidelines.

✈ **Gender:** Men and women may apply.

✈ **Citizenship:** In nearly all cases, you must be a U.S. citizen to work for a U.S. airline, or a Canadian citizen to work for a Canadian airline. If you are not a citizen, you must have a permanent work visa or resident alien card, also known as a green card. Because the supply of applicants exceeds the demand, few, if any, airlines will sponsor you to gain citizenship.

Your passport must not restrict entry to countries your airline serves. Not all airlines require passports but applying for one now will ensure that you are prepared when you need one. Application forms for passports are available at all U.S. and Canadian post offices, and can take at least two to three weeks to process.

For more information on obtaining a U.S. green card, visit the Immigration and Naturalization Service website at: http://www.ins.usdoj.gov/graphics/1GreenCard.htm.

✈ **Education:** You must be a high school graduate or have your general equivalency degree (G.E.D.). The airlines look favorably on at least two years of college, but it is not required.

✈ **Foreign languages:** All U.S. and Canadian airlines require flight attendants to be fluent in English. Most Canadian airlines also require fluency in French. Your chances of getting hired improve if you speak a second language such as French, German, Spanish, or Japanese.

✈ Chapter 5
EDUCATION

You will get nowhere with the airlines without at least a high school diploma.

All airlines require flight attendants to possess at least a high school diploma or a general equivalency degree (G.E.D.). If you're in school now, stay in school! If you've dropped out, go back and get your diploma or G.E.D. It does not matter if you speak five languages; **your application to become a flight attendant will be rejected if you do not have at least a high school diploma or G.E.D**.

Most airlines also prefer two years of college, largely for the maturity the college experience helps develop. A college education will also improve your chances of securing the job, in part because it reflects a desire to improve yourself. Courses that rate highly with the airlines include: sociology, psychology, history, geography, public speaking, math, and foreign languages. Be sure to list any applicable courses on your airline job application. Some community colleges even offer courses on how to become a flight attendant. And, while you're at it, be sure to take a course in first aid or cardiopulmonary resuscitation (CPR), which the American Red Cross offers in many cities.

Although few airlines formally require you to speak a language in addition to English (or in the case of most Canadian airlines, English and French), you greatly increase your chances of getting hired if you are fluent in several languages native to the countries an airline serves. Airlines also give preference to "language of destination" qualified persons when assigning flight schedules. For example, a French–speaking flight attendant is likely to receive priority to work Paris flights over a more senior flight attendant who does not speak French. You also usually receive additional pay for those flights. You

After reading this chapter, you would be prudent to learn the airline lingo in Chapter 20.

will be tested on your language ability, so list only the languages in which you are fluent — not the ones you've only begun to study. If you speak with a strong foreign accent, you may want to take some classes in public speaking. Because flight attendants are responsible for evacuating passengers in an emergency, passengers must be able to understand the attendants clearly — a pronounced foreign accent can undermine your role as an efficient safety instrument. Keep in mind that slang, gutter talk, jive, patois or street talk has no place in the aviation industry. If you find yourself saying things like "He ain't got no sense," you might want to reconsider this career move. You do not need to speak "the Queen's English," but you will need to speak standard American English with correct grammar while at work.

Many airline "schools" advertise that they will train you and place you with an airline. They tend to charge a fairly substantial fee or tuition for their services, sometimes as much as $2,000 or $3,000. Be careful; you probably do not need to attend one of these schools. Every airline will send you through its own training course, whether or not you have attended one of these airline schools, or have 20 years experience as a flight attendant at another airline. Everybody starts off on an equal footing. Prior flight attendant experience or training does not exempt you from training with your new airline, nor does it seem to give you any edge in getting hired by another carrier.

A select few charter airlines and most corporate flight operations require professional training. You will find further information on these schools and the courses they offer under the "Additional References" that begin on page 168 and in the chapter on corporate flying.

Carefully investigate any school that charges high tuition or promises placement with an airline. If you want formal preparation for a flight attendant career, stick to the inexpensive courses that adult education centers and community colleges offer. These courses can be found by exploring college catalogs or visiting the campuses in your neighborhood. But remember that the most you can get out of any of these informational courses is just that — information to help you decide if this is the right career for you.

✈ Chapter 6
LET'S GET PHYSICAL

All airlines will give you a physical examination before you complete training as well as a drug test that the Department of Transportation (DOT) requires. During your flight attendant career you will be subjected to random tests for drug and alcohol abuse. If you currently take illegal drugs, even on a sporadic or "recreational" basis, quit today! Your application will be rejected if you flunk the mandatory drug test. If you test positive for drugs or alcohol abuse once you are a flight attendant, you will be fired or grounded while you go through rehabilitation. Once you have been dismissed for flunking a drug test, chances are you will *never* work for an airline again!

You must be in good health with all your faculties functioning. Some health conditions that may disqualify you are high blood pressure, heart problems, chronic sinus, back, or hearing problems, and certain genetic and acquired syndromes. Your eyesight must be 20/20, or correctable to 20/20 with glasses, contacts, or corrective surgery. If you wear glasses, they should be conservative in size and style, with clear untinted glass.

Airlines require that you be at least 18 years old, although some set their minimum as high as 21. Not only does federal law prohibit airlines from discriminating on the basis of age, many airlines have recognized the benefits of hiring mature employees. It's not uncommon during training for a 19–year–old trainee to sit next to a 40– or 50–year–old trainee. People of all ages wish to travel the world as part of an airline crew. Many middle–aged applicants come to the job as a fulfillment of their lifelong dream to be a flight attendant, which may have been postponed due to marriage, family responsibilities, or child rearing. In fact, the airlines today prefer older applicants in part because

> **You should be in good physical condition because the work and hours of a flight attendant can be physically draining.**

they tend to have a better work ethic and be more stable employees.

Minimum and maximum height requirements are generally set at 5 feet, 2 inches, and 6 feet respectively, to ensure that a flight attendant is tall enough to reach emergency equipment and overhead compartments and short enough to fit into the smaller aircraft. Your weight must be in proportion to your height. Most airlines no longer adhere to strict height/weight charts, but look instead at the overall person. Space is limited in an aircraft, and being too large can prevent you from performing all your duties. Good physical conditioning is important because the work and the long hours are physically demanding. A typical meal service on a Boeing 777 aircraft can require making 100 to 200 trips up and down the aisles during a span of 90 minutes. This routine may be repeated two or three times in just one day. A flight attendant must also be physically able to open the aircraft doors, which can be quite heavy. You may also be called upon to carry passengers out of a burning aircraft, or to pull passengers out of their seats in order to perform cardiopulmonary resuscitation or operate an on–board heart defibrillator.

Airlines prefer pleasant looking applicants but not necessarily the *Vogue* model type. A clear complexion, no obvious facial scars, and neat, well–manicured hands are a must. Tattoos must not be visible while in uniform. Body piercing is prohibited except for pierced ears on women (and, at a few airlines, for men as well). Any other body piercing must not be visible while in your airline uniform. Earrings must be small and simple. Hair must be clean and styled — shoulder length for women and collar length for men. Longer hair is acceptable for women if it is tied back or worn up to meet sanitary requirements for handling food. Long hair is not acceptable for men. Some airlines allow beards and mustaches. Compliance with an airline's published grooming regulations is mandatory. Refusal to comply with published grooming regulations may lead to discipline or dismissal.

✈ Chapter 7
WORK EXPERIENCE THAT COUNTS

A previous job at Burger King will do more to get you hired as a flight attendant than experience as a certified public accountant.

The single best work experience you can bring to a flight attendant position is work that puts you directly in contact with the public. Dealing with the public takes practice, and you will need all the practice you can get before dealing with hundreds of people sealed in a tube hurtling through the air at 500 miles per hour! Working the counter at Burger King can enhance your chances of being hired as a flight attendant more than a career as a certified public accountant. List any public contact experience you have when you apply, no matter how trivial it may seem to you and strive to gain additional experience prior to your interview. Service work rates highly as well. This could be a job as a bartender, waitress, concierge, or caterer.

Airlines like flight attendants who take the initiative. Be sure to mention any volunteer work you've done since that shows initiative on your part. You will also want to include any awards or recognition you've received at your job or in your community. Other appropriate experience includes working in hotels, restaurants, retail sales, cruise ships, travel agencies, tour companies, customer service, car rentals, convention hosting, airport greeting, and hospital work. These types of jobs show that you can work with the same people with whom flight attendants work: the public.

Chapter 8

ATTITUDE, ATTITUDE, ATTITUDE

Two of the most important traits you will need to succeed as a flight attendant are flexibility and a positive attitude.

Succeeding as a flight attendant requires the diplomacy of a Nelson Mandela and the patience of a Mother Teresa. Passengers are in direct contact with flight attendants more than any other airline employee. So flight attendants can make the most lasting impression of the airline. Airline executives recognize that flight attendants are key employees largely because it is the flight attendants who are the single most responsible factor for repeat business, the bread and butter of the airline industry. Conversely, flight attendants with a bad attitude can drive away customers. These are among the key reasons why the airlines are so particular about whom they hire, and require their employees to follow the company guidelines for conduct and behavior.

Two of the most important traits you will need to succeed as a flight attendant are flexibility and a positive attitude. Flexibility is one of the requirements of the job that most flight attendants love, and it is the attribute you will need most to flourish on the job. If it is important to you to spend every night with your family or to watch "Wheel of Fortune," then this job is not for you. Being a flight attendant is not only a job; it's a lifestyle. It is possible you will have to work weekends when all your friends are off, and will be off work on weekdays when they are working nine-to-five. They will be able to live your travels vicariously but will not be able to join you on them in part because "free" travel benefits generally are available only to members of your immediate family, not to friends. In the first few years of your career as a flight attendant, it is very likely that you will have to work on all the major holidays, including Thanksgiving, Christmas, and Independence Day. You may miss weddings, birthdays, and special events. It will be difficult to make plans more than a month in advance, and even

> **This job will be either the most exciting career of your life, or the most disruptive event to your lifestyle.**

then you may be forced to change your plans at the whim of airline schedule changes.

Your spouse or significant other may not be able to accept your absence for days at a time. He may be jealous you have fun with new and interesting people, while he is left behind. If you have children, your care provider must be flexible and able to handle emergencies when you are 3,000 miles away, or stuck in a snowstorm halfway around the world. If you are a single parent, it can be especially difficult to secure childcare. Pets must be cared for in advance of your absence, either by leaving them with friends, or boarding them at your own expense.

And you may have to move to a new and strange city, far from your family and friends. This is especially true when you first start and are more likely to be assigned to a city that was not your first choice. While you can commute on your own airline (providing it serves your home town), you will be on an "on-call" basis when you first start flying, and will be required to be in your base city. You will need to factor in the costs of food and lodging since you are responsible for these expenses. Although this may sound severe, it's not much different than starting a new job with any company. The longer you work for an airline, the more seniority you acquire, and the more predictable your schedule will become.

The airline industry thrives on change, and you must be able to flow with the changes on a constant basis. If you need the predictability of a nine-to-five job, five days a week with weekends off, then this career is not for you. There is nothing routine when you are a flight attendant.

At this point, you must ask yourself, "Am I ready for this? Can I handle these changes and still keep my sanity?" This job will either be the most exciting career of your life or the most disruptive event in your lifestyle. It all depends on the attitude you bring to the job. Even though you may eventually have a somewhat regular work schedule, various uncontrollable factors such as weather, equipment breakdowns, and human illness and work stoppages will always keep your job as a flight attendant far from routine. A snowstorm in the Midwest can shift your layover in Hawaii to a layover in Des Moines. Your

Broom Hilda reprinted by permission of Tribune Media Services.
Copyright 1998. All rights reserved.

plans to get married one weekend could be dashed by an air traffic controller strike in Paris.

You must be flexible and positive during all unexpected in–flight "events" because passengers will look to you for guidance. When they are locked in an aircraft with you for hours, you are the lucky person on whom they will vent their anger and frustrations. This is where your diplomatic skills come into play. As a professional, you cannot get caught up in their mood and exacerbate a bad situation. You must convince them that everything will be fine, and leave them wanting to fly again on your airline.

✈ **Chapter 9**
CAREER BENEFITS

While your friends are shopping at local malls, you'll be shopping in Paris, Rome, or Hong Kong.

If you are flexible and able to accept change, the career of a flight attendant opens up unlimited possibilities. You may travel on your own carrier for free or a small service charge. Other airlines will give you discounts of 50 to 90 percent, and you will be entitled to discounts on hotel rooms, meals, tour packages, cruise ships and rental cars. These benefits may also extend to your parents, spouse, children, and in some cases brothers, sisters, and even friends! Plus, with the schedule flexibility that flight attendants have, you will also have the time off to enjoy these travel benefits.

You will regularly visit parts of North America and the rest of the world that some people only dream about. While your friends are shopping at local malls, you'll be shopping in Paris and Hong Kong. You can ski midweek when the prices are lower and there are no lift lines. You can ski the Alps! You can shop in Rome and dine in Paris. You will think of boarding a plane and flying to another city the way other people think of hopping on the bus to go downtown. Each month, you can usually schedule yourself a week or two off from work in addition to your annual vacation. In contrast, some nine-to-fivers only get one week's vacation a year!

As you gain seniority, you can schedule your flights so you can return to college, operate your own business, work a second job, or travel the world even more. Many airlines will regularly offer educational leaves of absence, maternity and paternity leaves, or extended leaves to pursue your new and varied interests. The opportunities are limited only by your imagination. Plus, you will come into contact with some of the most diverse and interesting people and cultures in the world. Some flight attendants have used their benefits to pursue travel photography, writing travel guidebooks, or visiting world historical sites. I know one flight attendant who organizes and

You may travel on your own airline for free or for a small travel charge.

leads safaris in Kenya each year, while another has used his time off to become a professional bass fishing guide.

A career as a flight attendant can also be your starting point for advancement into airline management. Your company will regularly post open job announcements within the airline before it looks outside the corporation. These include both permanent and temporary positions such as a flight attendant training instructors, supervisors, or interviewers.

In addition, most carriers offer comprehensive medical and dental insurance, as well as low–cost supplemental life insurance. These plans are also available to your spouse and children.

Nearly all airlines offer retirement plans with travel benefits for employees who have completed a minimum number of years of service. Profit sharing or stock investment plans may also be available.

Today's flight attendants see their profession as a way of life that encompasses not only their occupational opportunities, but also their personal lives. Essentially, your lifestyle is determined by the type of airline you select.

Your lifestyle is determined by the type of airline you select.

Scheduled Airlines: The bulk of a nation's airlines, including the smaller regional airlines, are scheduled airlines that publish regular flight schedules, with scheduled in-flight service to the general public. These scheduled flights operate at the same time every day or week, even if there is only one passenger on board. Tickets may be purchased up to the time of departure. United Airlines, Air Canada, ATA, and American Airlines are examples of scheduled airlines.

If you work for a scheduled airline, you get to choose your work days and hours a month in advance. Your choice may range from short or long trips, domestic or international, or a combination. These trips will vary little from month to month. If you are looking for the most stable and predictable work schedule, then a scheduled airline is the way to go.

Charter Airlines: A charter flight consists of an aircraft that has been contracted to fly from one city to another — usually by a third party. For example, a Minneapolis tour company may charter an aircraft to fly from Minneapolis to Miami each Friday during the winter. Minneapolis travel agents and tour companies will then sell the available seats to groups or individuals until the aircraft is filled. Other types of charters may be to carry a sports team between games, rock musicians to their next gig, politicians on their campaign circuit, or even flying the Pope on his Papal charter. Tickets are not sold at the airport, and must be purchased in advance. Passengers can only fly on the charter on which they are booked, and cannot transfer their tickets to another flight. The party that organizes the charter flight also determines the type of in-flight food and beverages.

Although charter flights have ticketing restrictions, they usually offer fares well below the cost of scheduled flights.

McDonnell Douglas DC9 (Narrowbody)

McDonnell Douglas MD80 (Narrowbody)

McDonnell Douglas DC10 (Widebody)

Boeing 727 (Narrowbody)

Boeing 757 (Narrowbody)

Boeing 747 (Widebody)

Airbus A320 (Narrowbody)

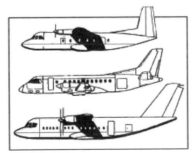

Commuter

FAA safety requirements are the same for charter and scheduled flights. While charter flights have ticketing restrictions, their fares are usually much less expensive than for scheduled flights. Charter flights may operate over regularly scheduled routes or over routes chosen by the booking party's needs. While many scheduled airlines also charter their aircraft, a charter airline flies only charter flights. American Trans Air, World Airways, and Ryan Air are examples of charter airlines.

Charter trips vary in length and destination, depending on the contract. They can even keep you away from home for weeks at a time. Your layovers can last for days in some pretty exotic locations. If a sports team or music group charters your aircraft, your layover may include box seats at the sports events or backstage passes to the concerts. Two of the most common and well–known charter contractors are military charters — transferring personnel and their families to and from military bases around the world, and the Haj — the annual flights of Muslim pilgrims to Mecca in Saudi Arabia. Because charter flights depend almost exclusively on the contracts received, their schedules are less regular and dependable. You may experience layoffs during slow periods. But charter flying will take you to places you may never get to see working for a scheduled airline.

Regional Airlines: These smaller commuter aircraft often serve smaller airports and destinations, and bring their passengers to the larger airports in order to connect with the major airlines. Many times these flights, though owned by separate companies, are operated under the jurisdiction of the larger airlines they serve. As a flight attendant for a regional airline, you would be able to use your free passes to travel on the partner airline. For example, if you work for SkyWest, ComAir, ASA, or Atlantic Coast, you would be able to travel on Delta Air Lines because these regionals are partners of Delta. United, Northwest, American, and USAirways all have similar arrangements. The aircraft may need just one or two flight attendants, or none at all.

United Express, Delta Connection and American Eagle Airlines are examples of regional airlines. Regional flights tend to be shorter, more local, and may originate and return on the same day, eliminating the need to keep flight attendants away from home overnight. If you don't want to be away for days at a time, or want to have the option of being home every night, then a commuter airline may be a better choice for you. Since they tend to be smaller companies with only a few hundred flight attendants, you will find more of a "we're all one big family" atmosphere. With the major airlines, which may employ 25,000 or more flight attendants, you may find yourself a small fish in a very big pond!

Corporate Flying: Many large corporations, such as IBM, 3M, and Exxon, own aircraft to fly their executives from place to place whenever needed, free of the scheduling limitations of commercial airlines. These jets may be as small as a Cessna, or larger than a Boeing 737. One or more flight attendants may be present on these jets, depending on the plane's size. Flight attendants who work for corporate airlines are usually on–call or available on a standby basis so they can be ready when a jet is needed. In addition to their in–flight safety duties, corporate flight attendants may also be required to procure and assemble the food and supplies needed for every flight, as well as cook the books (just kidding). Height limits may be lower because the smaller corporate planes have low cabin ceilings. Most corporate flight attendant recruiters prefer experienced flight attendants although training is available through private companies at the applicant's expense. A few of these schools are listed under "Additional References" beginning on page 168.

Much more information on corporate flying appears in the next chapter.

✈ Chapter 11
CORPORATE FLYING

A corporate flight attendant works on private, non–commercial aircraft. The corporate aviation world came into prominence shortly after World War II when a large supply of military transport aircraft and veteran pilots became available. As corporate air travel increased, so did the demand for a more business–oriented environment that would support the businessperson by providing total comfort and office amenities.

In the early days of business aviation, aviation managers and chief pilots usually used a male flight technician or mechanic in the back of the airplane as the acting third crew member. There was no emphasis on specialized or quality food service. Because interiors became increasingly detail–oriented in order to support the client's needs, so did the need to have a third crew member in the back of the aircraft who could also accommodate specialized culinary and amenity requests. The galley and cabin equipment became more elaborate and extensive as did the high–tech electronic communication and in–flight entertainments systems.

By the 1980s it became apparent that the third crew member needed to be an emergency and first–aid trained person with culinary skills. Now the corporate business traveler has privacy, anonymity, and a safe space to work in. Most importantly, they have the ability to create a non–structured time schedule that is changeable at any moment to suit their various needs.

There are three types of corporate flying: Part 91, Part 135 and Fractional.

✈ **Part 91** flying consists of private aircraft that are owned by individuals or corporations for their exclusive use.

✈ **Part 135** flying uses corporate jets, which are chartered to companies, sports teams, or individuals.

Corporate flyers offer flight attendants real opportunities.

✕ **Fractional jet ownership** came into existence in the late 1990s. Simply put, a corporate jet is shared by a few companies or individuals—each owning a time–share, or fraction of the aircraft use per month. This opens up the corporate jet option to a larger group of people, and has been the catalyst to make this the fastest growth sector in the industry.

The world of business aviation is a very exciting and ever–changing workplace. The challenges that are met to operate within this area of aviation are completely different from the commercial aviation arena. If there is any single character trait that is most important in this business called corporate aviation, it is flexibility.

It is important to emphasize that first and foremost, the safety of the passengers and the aircraft environment is paramount. When you consider your corporate client is paying from $4,000 to $6,000 per hour for the use of the corporate jet, excluding fuel burn ($30 per minute!) and food and catering costs, you can understand why corporate flight attendants must really excel in their work.

To succeed as a corporate flight attendant you need to be:

✕ Flexible

✕ Creative

✕ Accountable

✕ Honest

✕ Discreet

✕ Ego–free

A corporate flight attendant must also cultivate certain skills, including:

✕ High interpersonal skills

✕ Organizational skills

✕ Ability to take direction

✕ Attention to detail

- ✈ Effective time–management skills

- ✈ Listening skills

- ✈ Resolution skills

In addition to those skills just mentioned, as a contract or freelance corporate flight attendant, you must be able to:

- ✈ Book trips

- ✈ Maintain a cohesive monthly schedule

- ✈ Manage yourself as a business

- ✈ Interface with several flight departments

- ✈ Adapt to the standard operational procedures of different flight departments

- ✈ Always be open–minded

You must always be aware of, and remain on the leading edge of business aviation industry news and trends. You will do extensive research on the corporations you are flying for, including the corporate structure, the products or services they produce, as well as the companies they own. If you are flying the CEO of Coca–Cola on your jet, you surely don't want to order Pepsi products from your caterer, or even Frito's, which is a Pepsi–owned company. As with commercial aviation, the sources of this information can be found at your local library, on the Internet, and from such publications as *Business Week, The Wall Street Journal, The Economist,* and *The Financial Times.* It is recommended that you maintain this information in a database of your own design, so that you can review it in the event you fly the same client more than once. Client privacy and discretion are foremost, not only as a good business practice but also for the security of your client and flight. You can't blab to your friends that you are flying Donald Trump or Madonna around the country.

Like commercial aviation, a corporate flight attendant needs to be trained in safety, emergency procedures, and first–aid. However, some private corporate flight departments do not yet require this training. These operations place flight attendants

on–board as food servers and not as part of the
working crew. Advocates within the business aviation industry are working hard to require that *all*
flight attendants in corporate aviation receive corporate–specific training as part of the career. Until that
time, it is in your best interest to procure training on
your own if a corporate flight department does not
offer it. This training will make you much more mar-
ketable to those companies who only employ corporate–specific trained flight attendants. You should
have as much current business aviation and industry
training as possible, including:

- Corporate specific emergency and first aid
  training

- General corporate aviation training classes

- Service training classes

- Culinary training classes

Having as much industry training as possible will
allow you to act professionally within this specialized
venue of aviation should an emergency arise as well
as create a respect for your industry from the professionals in corporate/business aviation. You will find
an extensive listing of training sources under "Additional References" beginning on page 168.

Contract flying is some of the hardest flying you will ever do. It is without a doubt the most difficult area of flying for many reasons and the most rewarding for the same reasons! On a daily basis you find yourself interfacing within many diversified corporate cultures and the various personalities of many corporate flight departments. You must work with, and keep happy on every trip that you fly: the CEO, her corporate and personal family, the aviation manager, chief pilot, chief flight attendant, dispatcher, chief scheduler, chief of maintenance, the FBO staff, and caterers. In corporate flying, even more so than commercial flying, you are a vital part of the team. It is in the best interest of your company and clients for you to be highly trained and as prepared as possible. In the Appendix you will find listings of various training and fraternal organizations to assist you in pursuing this growing and exciting facet of the flight attendant career.

Author's note: My heartfelt thanks to Susan C. Friedenberg, president and owner of Corporate Flight Attendant Training, for allowing me to use portions of her copyrighted material in this chapter. Questions on becoming a corporate flight attendant can be emailed to Susan at scffatraining@aol.com or on her website at:

www.corporateflightattendanttraining.com

✈ Chapter 12
CHOOSING THE BEST AIRLINE FOR YOU

People frequently ask me, "Which is the best airline to work for?" Because of all the variables involved, I can't answer that question for you without knowing more about you and what is important to you. You have to answer it for yourself. I can give you some guidelines to consider when choosing the airline you would most like to work for.

Location: Do you want to stay where you currently reside? If so, you should look for airlines that have a domicile in your town. While there is no guarantee that you will be based there right out of training, you will at least have that option in the future. If they don't have a domicile in your town, then you will always have to commute to your domicile to begin your workday, and you may even have to travel there the day before and spend the night in a hotel at your own expense, just to ensure you can check-in for your working flight on time. If the airline you choose does not fly to your city, then you will have to pay your own way to get to the closest city they serve.

Or are you ready to explore new places and new locales? Perhaps you've always wanted to live in New York City, but cannot afford to move there without first having a job. You could select airlines that have flight attendant bases in JFK, EWR, LGA, or ISP. All these airports are within reach of the New York City area. Although it's not a common practice, you may have the opportunity to be based in a foreign country as part of your airline's crew. Or you may have friends who live in a particular city and would relish the chance to move there and live with or near them.

Schedule: Do you want to be home every night? Do you have children or a spouse, family, or significant other with whom you want to spend as much time as possible? Then you would want to concentrate on the regional carriers which usually have shorter flights and require fewer overnight stays.

If travel *is* what you desire, then the charter airlines would be a better choice. Their longer trips and foreign destinations will give you more layovers and interesting destinations. You may be gone for longer periods of time, but you will be seeing parts of the world that your friends can only dream of.

A compromise between the two is the most popular option, working for the scheduled carriers. An international airline can give you world travel on a regular and dependable basis. A domestic airline will give you shorter trips within your country.

Skills: Do you speak a foreign language? Then choose the airlines that fly to destinations where your language skills would be an asset. If you're a resident alien from Germany, you might choose an airline with flights to Germany so you can easily visit your relatives.

Interests: Are you a South American history major? Do you collect Asian Art? Are you a professional surfer, rock climber, runner, or biker? All these are things to consider when choosing your ideal airline. Once you have chosen the airlines that best meet your desires, you can go to their websites, investigate the companies further, and refine your choice.

Highest Pay: This is actually the last reason to choose an airline. As stated throughout this guide, there are no guarantees in this industry. You may start working for the airline that pays its flight attendants the highest salary in the industry, only to have your salary reduced by cutbacks or pay cuts due to slumps in the industry, bankruptcy, or corporate takeover. If you live in an area with a low cost of living, and choose an airline that pays more but requires you to live in an area with a high cost of living, such as New York, or San Francisco — then your higher salary is lost to food and lodging. Keep in mind that just because an airline pays more, it's not necessarily a better company to work for.

So which is the best airline to work for? The one that *you* choose to best meet your personal needs, skills, and interests.

✈ Chapter 13

THE APPLICATION PROCESS

Competition is fierce in today's airline environment. New applicants need to be better prepared than ever. You must do your homework!

The year I was hired as a flight attendant, my airline received 100,000 applications, interviewed 10,000 candidates, and hired 1,000 flight attendants. Translated into simpler terms, only one of every 100 applicants was hired.

That was in 1976, when airlines were enjoying a hiring boom. In today's airline hiring environment, you must compete with experienced flight attendants who have been laid–off or furloughed from their airline due to cutbacks after September 11. This means the competition is even fiercer, and new applicants must be better prepared than ever. You must do your homework and be better informed about what the job entails and how to best prepare so you will shine in the interview.

Take the time to apply the criteria you developed in Chapter 12 to the information about each airline in Chapter 25. Look closely at the domiciles, salary rates, languages required, etc., to narrow down your choice to about a dozen airlines. Then visit the websites of these select airlines to evaluate the routes they fly. You can learn about their growth potential and their position and strength in the industry from such business publications as *The Wall Street Journal, The Financial Times, The Economist* and *Business Week*. If you speak a foreign language, you will want to target airlines that fly to those parts of the world.

Do not apply to an airline whose qualifications you do not meet. If you are six feet tall, do not apply to American Eagle Airlines which sets its maximum height for flight attendants at 5 feet, 10 inches. No matter how qualified a candidate you are, no airline will make an exception for you. The first application screening process looks for compliance with the airline's standards. If you

FLIGHT ATTENDANT EMPLOYMENT APPLICATION

Airlines are most interested in your character.

do not comply, your application will be tossed out before anyone reads further. By all means do not lie or exaggerate facts on your application, hoping to win them over in the interview. If caught, you will not be considered, no matter how innocent the lie. As part of the hiring process, your airline will conduct a 10–year background check of your work history, schooling, and credit history. If you are caught with inaccurate information in your application, your chances of that airline hiring you will vanish. These background checks have taken on new importance since the terrorist events of September 11, 2001. However, if an airline's minimum age is 21 and you are 20½, say so. An airline will still consider your application as long you meet the minimum age requirement of 21 by the time you complete training.

Once you have narrowed down your list of potential airlines, send for an application using the addresses shown in the listings in Chapter 25. The websites of many airlines now have an online application form, and a few conduct the first interview by telephone. Some airlines may require you to send a self–addressed, stamped envelope (SASE) which they will use to return an application to you. To do this, you address an envelope to yourself, usually an 8½–inch by 11–inch envelope to avoid having to fold the application form. Affix the proper amount of postage for at least two ounces. Then fold and insert this envelope into another envelope that is addressed to the airline's application address. The airline will insert its application form into the SASE and drop it into the mail to you.

Airlines will look at any jobs you've held, your education, and any additional efforts you've made to better yourself.

If the airline requires a resume, send a professional–looking resume, with a cover letter. Your cover letter should be enthusiastic, sincere, personal, and explain why you chose this carrier over others. Specify the position you are seeking in your cover letter and use your cover letter to point out the items in your resume that make you well–qualified for the flight attendant position. Your resume should include your professional experience, education, talents, abilities, and languages spoken. Keep your resume down to a single page, certainly no more than two pages. You can find a number of excellent books on writing effective resumes and cover letters, as well as software applications for preparing your resume, in the online *Job Quest Catalog* at http://jobfindersonline.com.

For the airlines that do not require a resume, the choice is yours whether or not to send one. Some airlines look at them, others discard them. In the initial inquiry, many airlines are only looking for an address to which to send an application. A few airlines charge an application fee of $10 to $25 to help defray the costs of processing the thousands of applications they receive. This fee is non-refundable, and will have to be paid again if you reapply with that airline.

When completing an airline's application, print or type your answers legibly and neatly. Illegible or hastily scribbled applications are rejected first. It is a good idea to make a photocopy of the application when you receive it and use that copy for writing your first rough draft. Make sure that the information you enter fits into the space provided, so you do not have to write in the margins of the page. Be sure to go back at least ten years in your work and school history, because the airline will verify this information when it conducts its background check on you, as required by the FAA, when you are hired. Include contact names, phone numbers, and the full address for every employer. If a former employer is no longer in business, give as much information as you had when you worked there. Don't omit employers who fired you, or jobs you quit under bad circumstances — the background check will uncover them and you'll have some explaining to do, if the airline even gives you a chance to explain!

When everything fits in the spaces provided, clearly print the information on the actual application form you intend to submit. When you have finished filling out the application form, photocopy the finished application, and store your copy in a file folder for that airline. When you go for your interview, bring this photocopy with you as a backup, in case they lost the one you mailed.

Airlines are most interested in your character. They look at the types of jobs you've held, how long you've been in each, and your reasons for leaving. They look at your education and any additional attempts you have made to improve yourself. For this reason, along with your work and education history,

> **Talk to employees who work for the carriers that interest you. Learn as much as possible about the airlines to which you are applying.**

> **You must be patient and expect a delay of several weeks or longer after you submit your application.**

> **You are ahead of the game if a prospective airline is aware that you understand the job and its duties.**

list everything you've done that might be applicable to the job. For example, include in your resume outside activities such as volunteer or charity work, awards or special honors you've received, and first–aid or CPR courses you have taken. Emphasize experience you may have had working with the public. If you know somebody who works for the airline to which you are applying or who is a flight attendant for another airline, ask him to write a letter of recommendation for you to include with your application. She should know you well enough to be able to speak of your abilities and attributes should her supervisor contact her for more information. These letters of recommendation from people in the industry are a big asset in your interview — they tell the interviewer you are aware of the job duties of flight attendants, due to your interaction with this employee, and that you don't think it's all about serving coffee to movie stars. Include photocopies of the letters with your application, and bring the originals to your interview, along with any other non–airline letters of reference you may have.

Be sure to sign your application form where indicated. Follow any special instructions, such as returning the application by mail, or bringing it to the interview. Some airlines use this as a test of your abilities to follow instructions. Attach your photo only if the airline specifically requests one. Your photograph will come into play during the interview. Your photo should be a professional–looking "head and shoulders" portrait shot. Avoid using casual snapshots or "glamour shots."

It is prudent to maintain a log of the applications you mail, since you may need to reapply again in six months if you haven't had any response. Six months is the average time between applications. The actual time each airline retains your application can be found in the airline listings starting on page 81. Record the application date in your file and keep the extra copies of the airline's application form.

Some airlines will confirm receiving an application by sending you a postcard or an email. Others may not contact you at all. Most airlines will send a note informing you if they're not hiring at present, but will retain your application for a specified amount of time. Do not call or visit the local airline's office to monitor the hiring progress. The people you will speak to are far removed from the selection process and much too busy to be bothered by the thousands of applicants seeking flight attendant positions. Larger airlines interview thousands of applicants in various cities across their route system. From these groups of applicants, they select a few hundred to enter training classes with a dozen students in each class. This is a complicated and costly process for an airline to initiate, and for this reason, they may only interview and hire once a year. If an airline's hiring cycle comes in the spring and you apply in the fall, it may be six months before you receive a response to your application. During downswings in the industry, it may be years before an airline opens its hiring process again. You must be patient and expect a delay of weeks or even months when you submit your application for a flight attendant job. As you have probably realized, the hiring process for flight attendants is as unique as the job itself.

You should not consider it a waste of time to apply for an airline that isn't currently hiring. As indicated in the airline listings, most airlines will retain your application for an average of six months before discarding it. When an airline starts up its hiring process, these will be the first applications it looks at.

What can you do to enhance your chances of getting hired while you are waiting to be scheduled for an interview? Now is the time to do more homework. Talk to employees who work for the carriers to which you have applied. Try to learn as much as possible about these airlines. Read the business section of newspapers, industry magazines, and the Internet for news stories on the airline industry. Enroll in classes that will improve your chances of getting hired, such as foreign languages, public speaking, psychology, sociology, geography, public relations, or philosophy. Look to see if a local community college or adult education program offers classes on flight attendant or travel careers. You have a leg up on your competition if a prospective airline is aware that you understand the job and its duties. The initiative you show in taking these courses will reflect well on your sense of responsibility, setting you apart from the thousands of other applicants.

✈ Chapter 14
HOW TO SHINE AT THE INTERVIEW

The interviewing process for flight attendants is like no other interview you have ever experienced. Instead of a sedate review of your past work history conducted at the human resources office of a corporation, you may find yourself singing and dancing in front of a crowd of people! Because of this, the savvy applicant practices for interviews with his airlines of choice by attending interviews with airlines at which he does not intend to work. This practice will better prepare you for any question or situation an interviewer might throw at you. You can also gain valuable information by using the resources listed in the "Additional References" section in the back of this book, beginning on page 168. Knowledge is a valuable tool, and there is no such thing as too much interview knowledge.

Most airlines start the flight attendant interview with a road show group interview, or "cattle call." A large hall will be rented and groups of applicants will be given an overview of the airline and job requirements. Be sure to have all your resume information with you because you likely will be asked to complete a formal application at this time. One of the surest ways to be bumped from an interview is to say, "Can I get back to you on these dates? I don't have that information with me." If the airline had sent you an application, you should bring it with you, completely and neatly filled out, *before* you arrive at the interview. As explained in the previous chapter, you would be wise to photocopy the blank application form, so you can practice completing it, then put that information on the original copy as neatly as possible. You should also make a photocopy of the finished application, and bring it with you to your interview.

Always be as upbeat and positive as possible.

Following the "cattle call," small groups of applicants may be taken before a panel of interviewers. Further interviews may be given at that time or applicants may be notified about follow-up interviews by phone or mail. The second and third interviews may consist of groups of applicants meeting with a panel of interviewers, a single applicant meeting with a panel, or a one-on-one interview. Usually you will be sent a pass to travel on your prospective airline to interview in its training city. These "online" passes are good only on that airline's routes. If you don't live near a city your airline flies to, you will have to pay your own way to get to the closest city where that airline operates.

So what makes these interviews so different that brave people tremble at the mere thought of them? The fact is, the interviewers already know your personal history — it's on your application which has been pre-screened before you arrive. What the interviewers want to find out about you is your character:

- ✕ How do you handle stress?

- ✕ How well do you work as a team player?

- ✕ How do you take direction?

- ✕ How do you conduct yourself when faced with a difficult passenger situation?

- ✕ Are your social graces developed enough to fulfill the requirements of the job?

The interviewers want to discover your character, particularly how you handle stress.

These characteristics will be the focus of your interview. Consequently, interviewers are not necessarily going to ask you about your last job. They're going to put you in situations to see how you resolve them. For example, you may be asked to stand up on a stage in front of your group of applicants and sing the company's slogan, or invent a new one. They may give you an object, perhaps a pen or paper clip, and instruct you to "sell" it to the group. Many of these scenarios have no "right" or "wrong" solution. The interviewers do not expect you to know their specific corporate policies. Your answers show them how well you think on your feet and apply common sense in your solutions.

Airlines love to throw hard questions at you, to see how you react, such as:

Many successful applicants prepare for interviews with their airlines of choice by interviewing with other airlines just for practice.

- ✈ "You have such beautiful long hair. Would you cut your hair short to get this job?"

- ✈ "This job will require you to move to New York (or Des Moines, Walla Walla, Timbuktu). Will this create a strain on your relationship with your girlfriend?"

- ✈ "You will have to work every holiday for the next three years before you even have the possibility of getting a holiday off. Are you prepared for this?"

- ✈ "Why do you want to be a flight attendant?" [Do not answer this question with the standard reply "Because I love people and I love to fly!" Interviewers hear that response hundreds of times a day. A more effective answer would be to outline what you have to offer your prospective airline.] This is one place where your homework really pays off. Mention the new city that the airline is flying to, or the new candidate for CEO, etc. If you chose this airline for the chance to use your language skills, let them know that. Everyone being interviewed wants to be a flight attendant. The airline wants to know why it should choose you over the others. What skills will you bring to the airline to improve its position in the marketplace?

A smartly tailored, clean, pressed suit gives you a more businesslike appearance than a trendy or extreme outfit.

Let there be no doubt about it, pressure is placed on you to *perform* because there are no right or wrong responses. If you list a foreign language on your application, someone will test you, so you had better know more of the language than just "Buenos Días!"

Throughout the entire interview process, consider yourself on stage. It is common for an airline to evaluate you as you wait to be called into an interview session. One of your fellow applicants is often a company employee working undercover. She may talk with you before the interview and reveal that she "heard" the airline is not a good one to work for. Never speak negatively about the airline, or compare it to other companies in a conversation without another job candidate. They could be undercover employees who will convey your answers back to the company.

Some airlines even go so far as to ask the working crew how you behaved on the flight to the interview! They will be observing you to see how you get along with the other applicants. Did you mingle with other applicants and engage them in conversation; or did you sit off by yourself in a corner? A friendly and outgoing personality is better suited for this career than the shy, retiring type

Throughout your interviews, whether they are group, panel, or individual interviews, maintain good eye contact with the interviewer. And always, always, remember and use the interviewer's name. If you're in a group interview, remember the names of the other applicants and listen to what they're saying in their responses. Then use this information in your own responses, in a scenario much like this:

INTERVIEWER: "And what do you feel is the main reason for flight attendants on an aircraft?"

YOU: "Well, Jane, I agreed with Ralph when he said it's for passenger comfort, but I feel the most essential reason for flight attendants to be on board is passenger safety."

After the interview, be sure to thank your interviewer(s) by name. Reiterate to them how you would like to be a part of their in-flight team, and what you think is the key skill you would bring to the position. This will leave them with a good impression of you, which they will remember when deciding who continues on to the next level of the application process and who receives the rejection letter. If you get the opportunity, this is the time to attach a small photo to your application form or resume. It should not be much larger than two inches square and should be a professional-looking shot of your head and shoulders. Interviewers may talk with hundreds of applicants in a day and make notes on their applications. As they try to narrow down their choices at the end of the day, interviewers will review the applications that weren't immediately rejected. Having a photo on your application gives them a visual image that will help them remember your interview, and the impression you made.

> **It's a fallacy that airlines are seeking only people who look like fashion models.**

> **Perseverance is the key to success.**

Sometimes it's those tiny details that make or break you. As noted earlier, many airlines require you to complete an application at the interview. Let's say you forgot to bring a pen: you ask the interviewer for one and are given a pencil. Later, when the interviewers go through the applications, they will throw out the ones filled out in pencil. This little trick enables them to identify those applicants who showed up unprepared, and therefore are probably not very good at planning ahead for a given situation.

Are you friendly and talkative, or are you shy and keep to yourself? Your posture and how you sit, walk, and talk will all be checked. This information may be reported to the interviewers before you enter their office, or may be noted on your application form in a code the interviewers understand. Always be on guard at *all* times, not just when you are in front of the interviewers. Are you slumped against the wall or slouching in your seat while waiting to be called? Is this what you would consider "professional flight attendant" demeanor? Your interviewers will not! Be friendly, talkative, and sincerely interested in the people around you. Don't criticize the company or any other airline. Always be as upbeat and positive as possible.

Even if it is allowed, don't smoke during the interview process. All U.S. and Canadian airlines are now nonsmoking environments. One airline will not even consider applicants who use nicotine products. As a working crew member, you will have to comply with the same smoking restrictions as your passengers. So it's best to quit smoking now, before you apply or get hired.

Allow enough travel time to avoid arriving late. Interviewers close the doors to the interview room promptly at the specified time.

Interview attire is also important. A smartly tailored suit that is clean and pressed will give you a more businesslike appearance than a trendy or extreme outfit. Avoid wearing too much makeup; apply just enough to enhance your natural features. It's a fallacy that airlines seek only flight attendants who look like fashion models. They hire the complete person. Age, weight, height, and appearance standards have been relaxed over the years, making this career available to a larger cross–section of the public.

You should want to put your best appearance forward. Neat, recently trimmed hair (most men wearing beards will be asked to shave when hired), clean

hands and manicured nails (nail biters seldom get hired), a clear complexion, and a slim, well–proportioned figure are very important for both sexes. Women should wear small, simple earrings and avoid excessively large or dangling ear adornments. Men should not wear an earring, even though a few airlines may allow male flight attendants to wear a simple stud in their ear. Body piercing in other locations is unacceptable and should not be worn to the interview. Tattoos should not be visible when you are clothed. **Your appearance contributes to whether airline passengers will have confidence in you — and the airline wants flight attendants who inspire confidence in the passengers**. This is not a platform for you to express your beliefs or style ideas. Airlines are looking for a *uniform* appearance.

A lot has been written lately about weight requirements. Recent lawsuits against airlines by older flight attendants required to maintain their hiring weight well into their mature years have been settled in favor of the flight attendants. Now airlines simply say that weight must be "in proportion to height," as opposed to following strict height/weight charts. It will, however, improve your chances at the interview if your body is in good physical condition. Remember, a flight attendant's primary function is safety. So it is quite reasonable for an airline to require its flight attendants to be physically fit. Be forewarned that it is very easy to gain weight while working as a flight attendant. Maintaining a regular schedule of exercise can be difficult. Therefore, it is imperative that you begin now to control your weight and physical condition.

The appearance criteria may be very subjective. Every airline looks for a different type of person. Some want the all–American look, others want the sophisticate. Still others will want the characteristics most traditionally associated with the regions in which they operate. Each company and each interviewer for that company has a different interpretation of what will fulfill their needs. It's not unusual for an applicant to be turned down by an airline one day and hired by another the next. A major carrier rejected a friend of mine three times before hiring him on the fourth try.

Your interviewer is usually a flight attendant on special assignment who is not a professionally trained interviewer. It may come down to five excellent candidates and only four openings. This is where all the little things you do in the interview make or break you. If you are rejected, turn this disappointment into a positive learning experience and go on to interview with other carriers.

If you do not hear from an airline within a couple of weeks after the interview, you have not been accepted for training. Do not become discouraged or take it personally. Sometimes the personal preferences of the interviewer subconsciously affect her judgment. Perhaps he does not like blondes, New Yorkers, or Albert Belle fans.

Perseverance is the key to success. If you are turned down by an airline, you will rarely be told why. Any attempts to discover why you were rejected will probably fail. Keep in mind that an average interview series can have hundreds of applicants, and that the interviewers travel to many cities to conduct these interviews. Speaking with the decision makers can be next to impossible. Many career counselors routinely advise sending a "thank you" note to interviewers. But this does not make much sense for flight attendant applicants because of the nature of the interviewing process. Connecting the note with your application or your interviewer may be impossible. Simply accept the loss of this application window, move on, and apply to that airline again at your next eligible date.

You would be prudent to bring the following items to your interview:

- ✖ Social Security card
- ✖ Passport
- ✖ A certified copy of your birth certificate
- ✖ Copies of your resume
- ✖ All the information needed on the application (this could be your resume)
- ✖ Letters of reference
- ✖ Alien registration and work permit (if you are not a citizen of the country where the airline is hiring)
- ✖ Pen
- ✖ Watch

Allow adequate travel time to avoid arriving late. Interviewers will close the doors to the interview room promptly at the specified time. If you are even a minute late, you will either be denied entrance until the next session, or will be allowed to enter — though you now have two strikes against you.

Why this test? Airlines operate on strict schedules. You must be punctual and reliable if you want to work in this industry. This is *not* the career for you if you are habitually late. In fact, if you are even five minutes late more than once for your flights, you are fast on your way to looking for a new job. So, as the interviewers see it, if you can't arrive at the interview on time, how likely is it that you will be on time for the flights you work?

A few airlines, including United, have started to give successful interviewees a written test before making a final hiring decision. You would be prudent to check in advance with any airline that interviews you to learn if flight attendant candidates must take a written test and, if so, what the test covers.

✈ Chapter 15
CONGRATULATIONS: YOU'RE HIRED!

You may find out at the interview, or you may be notified weeks later by mail, that your chosen airline has selected you and scheduled your training class date. It will send you a large packet with the information needed to prepare you for what will be expected of you as an employee in your new career. You will also receive additional application and insurance forms, as well as a basic home study course to start your preparation for work as a flight attendant. You are expected to learn this information *before* arriving at the training academy. Study and memorize the material that is sent to you, which may include such subjects as: the 24–hour clock; world time zones; Greenwich, or "Z" time; your airline's route system; basic airline terminology; and a brief history of the company. Also included in the packet will be a listing of the three–letter airport codes for the cities your airline serves. Every commercial airport in the world is identified by these three–letter codes. To eliminate any possible confusion or duplication, no two airports are assigned the same code, nor can the code look or sound similar to that of any other airport within a range of two hundred miles. You will need to memorize these airport codes before you start training since you are usually tested on them first. To help you get started, see the listing of the most common airport codes in chapters 21 and 22.

Many of these codes are easy to remember, such as DAY (Dayton), PIT (Pittsburgh), BOS (Boston), and MAD (Madrid). Others can be very confusing, such as FCO (Rome), BNA (Nashville), ORD (Chicago's O'Hare Field), TXL (Berlin), and CVG (Cincinnati). Some airlines will terminate your employment and send you home from training if you don't pass this first test.

Some airlines will terminate your job and send you home if you fail this first test.

✈ Chapter 16
TRAINING

The FAA requires flight attendants to be on board for only one reason: passenger safety.

Pay careful attention to the date on which training begins. Airlines must schedule training classes well in advance, so your training may start within a week of being told you've been hired or as long as six months later. Upon notification of your proposed training date, allow time to attend to personal affairs. Since most training classes run five weeks, you should arrange with someone back home to handle your affairs while you are in training. Who is going to take care of your pets and water your plants while you're gone? Who is going to forward your bills and mail to you at the training center? Ensuring that these things are taken care of will ease your mind, and allow you to concentrate on your training material. If you are currently employed, give your employer two to four weeks notice. Allow adequate time to get your life in order and to study your pretraining materials. Unless your training is in your hometown, plan on remaining at the training facility for the entire duration of your schooling.

On rare occasions, training classes have been canceled or postponed due to circumstances beyond an airline's control. Good examples of this are the Gulf War of 1990–1991, and the aftermath of the September 11, 2001, terrorist attacks. Passenger air travel decreased so much during these events that many airlines had to cut back on personnel. If you had been awaiting your training date, your airline would have postponed or even canceled training. In some cases, it took a year to reschedule training classes. Fortunately, these occurrences are not common.

You will be tested on safety information time and again.

Training is held in the airline's home city or hub, generally the same location where you mail your application form. Most airlines provide either lodging for trainees, or will help you find suitable lodging at local hotels with which they contract for this purpose. Some will pay you a salary when you start training, others when you successfully complete it. Some airlines pay you only a per diem for food and

The lives of the passengers and crew depend on how well the flight attendants are trained.

expenses. In many cases, you will have to pay for your food and lodging yourself — tax deductible expenses — so keep your receipts and consult your tax advisor. Chapter 25 provides this information for each airline. Regardless of what the airline offers, you would be prudent to arrive at training with enough funds to cover food and expenses for the three– to six–week training period.

Pack enough clothing. Business attire is required while in the classroom and common areas of the training center. More casual clothes and even a swimsuit may be required for training in evacuation and wet ditching or water landings. The training center may provide laundry facilities, or you may need to use a local laundromat.

You will usually share a room with one to three other trainees. But for the next three to six weeks, the flight attendant training academy will be your home away from home, the place where you are transformed into a professional flight attendant. Instructional facilities are usually modern and multifaceted, although their nature varies with each airline. A few of the smaller airlines may use an airline training facility in another city when they have none of their own. You will also notice in the airline listings in Chapter 25 that some airlines conduct training in more than one city.

Classroom training is usually conducted from 8 a.m. to 5 or 6 p.m., six days a week. If you live in the city where training is held, you may be allowed to spend your nights at home. Otherwise, plan to be at your training center the entire time. If you become homesick and wish to fly home for a visit, the airline may give you a pass to get home but may not allow you to return. There are thousands of applicants willing to take your place, and no reason for an airline to make special arrangements for any student. Exceptions to this policy are made only for trainees who become seriously ill or unable to continue training for reasons beyond their control. Once you are able to return to training, you will be worked into the next available class. If training sessions have already been completed by the time of your return, you will have to wait until your airline begins training again.

The federal government requires that you be fully trained in safety for every type of aircraft your airline operates.

The general flying public believes that a flight attendant is on board an aircraft only to serve coffee

Seniority governs your whole career as a flight attendant.

Airlines value dependability in their flight attendants very highly.

and food. But the Federal Aviation Administration (FAA) regards meal service and airline public relations as secondary duties. **The FAA requires flight attendants on all passenger flights for only one reason: passenger safety.** Flight attendants have been called upon to render first aid for cuts, bruises, burns, choking, airsickness, and even broken bones. Flight attendants have even helped with childbirth and thwarted hijackings.

The federal government requires you to be "safety trained" for every type of aircraft your company operates. You will be forbidden to work on an aircraft for which you have not been trained and tested. You will be retested annually. Failure can mean loss of duty time or your job. You will need to know the type, number, location and use of the fire–fighting equipment on board, including the newly installed smoke hoods. Competence is also required in operating all emergency exits and evacuation techniques. Basic first aid, CPR and oxygen administration, and anti–hijacking techniques are also part of flight attendant training.

Most of the typical training day is spent learning and being tested on these safety requirements. You will receive hands–on training with the oxygen, fire–fighting, and first–aid equipment. In a mock-up of an actual aircraft, you will practice evacuating a simulated flight, complete with darkness, smoke, unusable exits and "injured" or disabled passengers played by your classmates or instructors. Training may even require you to jump into a swimming pool to give you real–life practice at water landings. This would include donning and inflating your life vest, inflating a 40– to 60–passenger life raft and making it secure, retrieving swimming "passengers," and signaling for rescue aircraft. The remainder of your classroom training will consist of company policies and procedures, the paperwork required for every flight including customs and immigration forms, and dining and service flow.

Be prepared to relocate when you enter training, remembering the potential cost factors of moving to a new city.

Many flight attendants and pilots commute from the cities they live in to their respective domiciles.

Training time will also be spent on how to operate the in–flight movie system, duty–free sales on international flights, and the elaborate food and beverage services in first class and coach. Your classmates will act as passengers as you learn how to set up, cook, and serve meals and drinks from aisle serving carts in a professional and pleasing manner. You will also learn how to clean up and stow everything away again before landing.

To achieve FAA certification, every airline must demonstrate that its crews can evacuate an entire aircraft filled to capacity in 90 seconds or less — with only half of the available exits functioning. The lives of the passengers and crew depend on how well you implement your safety training. Your airline, therefore, will concentrate heavily on safety. You will be tested repeatedly on this information, and you must be proficient in all of it to complete training and begin flying.

You will be required to score 90 percent or better on most of the daily and weekly tests administered during training. Your airline already has a lot invested in you, and has chosen you because you have what it is looking for — so it is going to work with you to ensure you complete training successfully. However, the airline will not hesitate to send you home if you just cannot grasp the material or are not willing to comply with the rules and requirements it has established.

Bring a flashlight with you to training since the FAA requires all flight attendants to carry a flashlight at all times while on duty. The "Mini–Maglite™" type has become the flashlight of choice among flight attendants. The ***Emergency Procedures Manual*** *(EPM)* your airline issues to you is also required equipment, and you are responsible for keeping it current with the revisions you will constantly receive in your company mailbox. This manual serves as your constant guide to company rules, regulations, handling unusual situations, and emergency procedures. You can be fined $500 if an FAA spot check finds you without your flashlight or a current *EPM*. A reliable, working watch, conservatively styled of course, is also a necessity.

When you finish training, you will be fitted for your uniform and accessories. Each airline has its

> **Some airlines give you travel privileges when you complete your training.**

own style of flight attendant uniforms. Airlines employ leading fashion designers to create uniforms for their flight attendants that are durable, practical, and versatile, yet still fashionable. Your uniform makes you easily recognizable in an emergency situation where you have to exercise leadership. The uniform also sets flight attendants apart as the people responsible for providing service and comfort.

In most cases, you are expected to purchase your first uniform, although some airlines split the cost with you. The average $500 cost is deducted from your paychecks during your first year of employment. The airline generally pays for all replacement uniform items. When on duty, you are expected to be in full uniform. Even though you may wear business attire when you fly on a company plane in a non-working capacity (known as "deadheading"), there is no excuse for not having a complete and clean uniform on hand before each trip.

While in uniform, flight attendants must maintain a professional manner and appearance. This rule applies not only on the airplane and in the airport terminal, but also while in uniform on public transportation and in layover facilities. For example, you cannot enter a bar or liquor store while in uniform, even after you have completed your workday and are on your way home. The people who see you might think that you are drinking on your way to work, and this reflects badly on your company's image of safety and security. To maintain a uniform appearance, you are not allowed to substitute your own clothes, or accessorize your uniform to suit your personal tastes. It is your responsibility to maintain your uniform with tailoring, dry-cleaning or laundering at your own expense. Fortunately these expenses are tax–deductible if you keep proper receipts.

"**Seniority**" rules in almost any work–related situation in the airline industry. When you graduate from training, you will be assigned a seniority number that gives you a rank among all other flight attendants flying for your airline on a systemwide basis. This number can be determined by your age in training, or by the last four digits of your Social Security number. For example, the most senior person in a class of 40 students has 39 people below her in seniority. Each successive class of trainees will increase the number of people below you, therefore making you more senior. However, if you are starting with one of the major airlines, thousands of people probably will be your seniors. As the people above you resign or retire, you move up the seniority list. There are two types of seniority: System Seniority which is your ranking with all of the flight attendants in the company; and Relative Seniority, which is your seniority in your crew base if your airline has more than one crew base.

You accrue flight attendant seniority as long as you remain on active flying status. Most companies allow their flight attendants to continue to accrue seniority during leaves of absence and while on special assignment with the company or union. If you leave one airline to work at another, you forfeit all your rights as a flight attendant, including your seniority status. In other words, if you have five years seniority with United Airlines, and you go to work for American Airlines, you will start all over again with zero seniority. Similarly, if you leave American Airlines after accruing five years seniority and reapply a year later, you will again start with zero seniority.

After training, you may be allowed to select from your airline's base cities the city from which you will begin and end all your flights, or your airline may simply assign one to you depending on its needs when you graduate training. This city will be your **"home base station,"** or **"domicile."** Some airlines have only one domicile for flight attendants; others have as many as 12. Not all cities will be available to you. Some domiciles are more senior than others — in other words, more preferred. Given a choice of Des Moines or San Francisco, where would *you* prefer to live? More people senior to you are likely to select San Francisco as their domicile, thereby making it a more senior base. You will start in a "junior" domicile, but can transfer to a more senior domicile at a later date when your *System Seniority* has risen.

You are initially assigned your domicile for a specific period of time, usually six months, before you can request to be transferred to another. Your transfer request will be processed in seniority order. If you are not senior enough for a particular base, or if there are no openings there, your request will be denied. It may take many years of service with your

Photograph of Pan American steward serving passengers
reprinted by permission of Helen McLaughlin.

airline before you are based in some of its more senior domiciles. This is one of the reasons airlines ask if you are willing to relocate. If you don't get assigned the base of your choice after training, you can always quit and go home, but don't waste your time applying to that airline again. As mentioned earlier, even though you may be fully trained, other airlines don't recognize that training, nor do they give hiring preference to you if you are. And if you tell them you left your last airline because you did not get your domicile of choice, then this other airline will not want to hire you either.

Many flight attendants and pilots commute from the cities they live in to their respective domiciles. My airline has New York–based flight attendants commuting from as far away as Hawaii and Israel. Many commuters will share a "commuter apartment" in the domicile when they are spending a night or two between trips. Four to six commuters can easily share a two–bedroom apartment and seldom see their fellow roommates because their work schedules are so different. All commuting is done at your own expense and is not considered an excuse for arriving late for your assigned working flight. You will have to use your airline's pass system for commuting, and you may only have a limited number of passes per year. Other airlines will sell you reduced rate tickets, but these may cost you $100 or more per commute.

When you multiply that by four or five trips in a month, the expense can add up quickly. In all cases, you will be traveling on standby and are not guaranteed a seat. If you are "on reserve," you must live in your base city during the days you are on call, since you may be given only an hour's notice to appear for a flight.

Airlines look very closely at dependability. An aircraft cannot depart if it is not fully staffed. A missing or late flight attendant can be very costly to hundreds of passengers as well as to your airline. Again, if you are constantly late for appointments, this is not the career for you. Excessive incidents of illness, tardiness, or missed flights can lead to discipline or dismissal.

After you complete training, you may be given time to return home before starting work in your new city, or you may start working right away. You should be prepared for both possibilities when you enter training. Keep in mind the potential cost factors of moving to a new city. You may share an apartment in your new city with the friends you made while in training, or move in with family or friends. Thanks to different flight schedules, you and your new roommates may seldom be in the apartment at the same time. Some airlines give you travel privileges when you complete training, others wait until you complete your probationary period. Again, this period of probation is a time when you must be extra diligent. Any infraction of the rules, such as missing a flight or showing up late, can be cause for immediate dismissal.

✈ Chapter 17
FLIGHT SCHEDULING

After completing training, you will be assigned to one of your airline's domiciles for flight attendants.

The FAA limits the maximum number of hours a flight attendant can fly each month. **Flight hours** consist of the time from when an aircraft leaves its airport gate (**block out**) to when it arrives at the next airport gate (**block in**). Your salary is based on block hours every month, with the minimum number of hours varying with each airline. Each airline's salary scale, based upon minimum flight requirements, appears in Chapter 25. Flight attendants average 70 to 75 block hours of work every month.

"What a job!" you say, after looking through the airline listings in Chapter 25. "I'm used to working 40 hours every week!" This is a common misconception lay people share. While you will receive flight pay for 75 hours in a typical month, you will be away from home 250 to 300 hours, and will actually work an average of 14 to 20 days each month. Time spent on the ground during preflight, boarding, and deplaning is time for which you will be paid only at **per diem** rates, if at all. You not paid when you are in a layover city overnight. To help with food expenses, you may also receive a per diem for the time you are away from home.

In most cases, when you complete training, you will be assigned to one of the domiciles your airline has established for its flight attendants. Again, your airline may allow you to select your domicile or it may assign you to one.

You will be assigned a **reserve line of time** for your first month. This means you will be on call, and must be packed and ready to leave on a moment's notice. You may be allowed to wait at home, or you may be required to wait in full uniform at the airport. When another flight attendant calls in sick, is late, or is otherwise unable to work her flight, a **reserve** will be called to fill the opening. The FAA specifies the number of

| January |||||||
Sun	Mon	Tue	Wed	Thu	Fri	Sat
	1	2	3	4	5	6
7	8	9	10	11	12	13
14	15	16	17	18	19	20
21	22	23	24	25	26	27
28	29	30	31			

Flight attendants "bid" for specific flights every month.

Most airlines prefer to hire from within to fill openings for in–flight supervisors, trainers, and instructors.

flight attendants that must be on a given aircraft, and the aircraft cannot depart until this number is met. Your ability as a reserve to make it to the airport on time may determine whether or not a flight filled with passengers leaves as scheduled — yet another reason why airlines stress punctuality during the interview process.

The longer you work for an airline, the more seniority you will accumulate. This seniority will eventually be sufficient to enable you to get off reserve and **hold a line of time.** Each month a listing of scheduled flights is distributed to the flight attendants in what is called a **bid package** consisting of **flight pairings** or trips spaced out through the 30 days that make up a bid month, or **sequence**. Each individual pairing will indicate when the trip begins and ends, and every flight leg you will work in the sequence. It will also indicate where you will spend the night if you have an overnight or **layover** and how long your layover will be. A pairing may be for an entire crew on that trip, or it may only be for you, working as a **fill–in** or **extra** flight attendant. Each sequence is different from the others in the type of trips, layovers, and destinations.

You may choose your preferred trips because of the length of the trip, the destinations, the length and/or location of layovers, the days off from duty, or the number of days away from home. These trips may consist of multi–day flight pairings, or **turnarounds**, which depart and return on the same day with no overnight stay. The pairings are usually spread throughout the month and may be two–on–three–off (two days on duty followed by three days off duty) three–on–two–off, back–to–back (flights scheduled one after the other, allowing only minimum rest between each), or any combination of trips, short or long. The FAA sets minimum standards for **legal rest** from duty.

When **bids** close, all bid requests are tallied in seniority order, and you are given your schedule for the next month. If you are not senior enough to hold a line, you will be scheduled into the reserve pool. Reserve lines are posted in the same manner as the lines for regular line–holders and the process of bidding is similar except that reserves bid for days off rather than trip sequences.

As a reserve, you are guaranteed payment for a specified number of credited hours, whether or not you fly that many hours. You may find yourself not flying at all in a given month, yet you will still be paid for the minimum monthly hours. Most airlines allow reserves to use a pager or cell phone — at their own expense, of course — for those periods when they are on call.

Most airlines allow line holders to trade flights to rearrange your schedule more to your liking. If you need a specific weekend off for a concert, one of your co–workers may be willing to trade trips so you can attend. Some airlines even allow **job sharing** where you can split your month with another flight attendant and fly only half as many days or hours — a valuable benefit for flight attendants who are parents or also students. Remember, though, that if you work only half a month, you earn half pay.

Seniority is your whole life in the airlines. It dictates which trips you fly, what position you work on the aircraft, when you take your vacation, and when you get pay raises. If you switch airlines, you lose all seniority and start again at the bottom of the pecking order at your new airline — a practice that makes changing airlines in mid–career very unappealing.

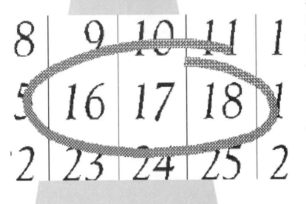

✈ Chapter 18
A TYPICAL THREE–DAY TRIP

Although each airline has its own service nuances, the flight attendant's daily routine is basically the same at all airlines. This chapter outlines a typical three–day trip.

You begin by reporting for duty at your domicile airport, in full uniform and fully packed, at least one hour prior to your scheduled flight departure, to check–in, or notify the airline that you are in position to begin your trip. If you fail to check–in, a reserve may be called to take your place because your airline thinks you are a **no–show** — yet another reason interviewers are so concerned about punctuality. You will meet with your fellow crew members, some of whom you may be meeting for the first time. A crew briefing usually follows, and may include bidding for the position on the aircraft that you will working. You can also check your company mailbox for any notices or materials from your airline, or even notes from your flying friends. You can also receive a trip manifest that highlights any special passengers you may have, such as passengers with disabilities, sky marshals, unaccompanied children whom you must care for, or even celebrities.

You will board the aircraft approximately 45 minutes before the scheduled departure time. Once on board, you will stow your gear in the proper manner and perform a **pre–flight check** to make sure that all emergency equipment is in its assigned location and in working condition. In training, you learned the locations and operation of all the emergency equipment for all of the types of aircraft your airline operates. The absence of some emergency equipment

At 30,000 feet, you can't run out to the store to get the food or drinks you need to serve your passengers.

can prevent an aircraft from departing until it is replaced, so this check is very important. If you have an oven fire, you need to react quickly, and you won't have time to pull out your *Emergency Procedures Manual* to discover where the closest fire extinguisher is stored. When the pilots have completed their own check–in, they board the aircraft and brief you on the anticipated weather for your flight route, and the expected altitude and time it will take to get to your destination. They may also advise you of any other unusual circumstances, such as inoperative equipment or special procedures.

If you are working the galley position, you will check food and supplies to ensure you have enough for the passenger load. When you are 30,000 feet above the ground, you cannot run out to the store to get the food or drinks you need to serve your passengers, so this inventory is very important! Did the caterers provide enough soft drinks, napkins, cups, snacks, coffee, silverware, entrees, etc.? In training, you learned what to look for, and what should be supplied. If a shortage is discovered, notify the lead flight attendant as soon as possible to allow time to obtain additional items.

You will want to prepare as much as you can in the galley before passengers start boarding to enable you to assist the flight attendants working in the cabin. When the passengers start boarding, you will assist by hanging first class passengers' coats, serving on–ground beverages, and helping passengers find their seats and proper locations to stow their carry–on luggage.

Some trips consist of only one leg a day, while others can have as many as seven to ten legs.

Once the aircraft's doors are closed, you complete your safety requirements by demonstrating the safety equipment and showing your passengers where the exits are located. Some aircraft use a video presentation for the "demo," but you must be preared to conduct a manual demonstration in case the video breaks down. Finally, you will visually check to ensure that all passengers have complied with safety requirements by buckling their seat belts; placing tray tables and seat backs in their full upright positions; turning off all personal electronic equipment such as cell phones, computers, radios, and CD–players; and stowing their luggage in overhead bins or under seats.

A 21–hour layover in San Francisco gives you time for dinner with the crew in one of the city's superb restaurants.

Now it's time to sit in your "jump seat" for take-off. During taxi and takeoffs, you mentally review your safety training. Visualize in your mind where your exits are located, how to operate them, and what to do if your closest exit is unusable. Review the location of your portable fire extinguishers, emergency light switches, and evacuation alarms if your plane is equipped with them. This **30–second review** provides an extra level of safety and has proven successful in emergency situations.

When the plane reaches cruising altitude, the captain will notify you whether the flight will be smooth and the flight attendants can start preparing the meal and/or drink service. The flight attendant assigned to work the galley will ensure that the meals are cooking properly while another flight attendant pulls out the beverage cart and stocks it with ice buckets, cups, napkins, and any other items needed for service. This cart is then taken out into the aisle to serve beverages, followed by a meal or snack service.

After all passengers have been served, flight attendants start retrieving the trays and glasses beginning with the front row. **Federal Air Regulations** prohibit loose articles such as cups, glasses, and other

Your first raise will come after six months to one year of service.

service items in the aircraft during landing. The drink cart that you had set up must now be "torn down" and everything stowed in its assigned place. Since your primary responsibility as a flight attendant is to ensure that **FAA Regulations** (FARs) are maintained, all loose items must be picked up and stowed in their proper places prior to landing. After conducting a final check on your passengers, you will buckle up for landing and once again conduct a "30–second review" of safety procedures. You help passengers deplane, then may tidy the aircraft after they've gone. New food and supplies are brought on board, and the cycle begins again for the next portion, or **leg** of the flight.

Some trips may have only one leg a day; others may have as many as seven to ten. You must appear as fresh and friendly on the seventh leg as you did on the first. A workday may range from a few hours to ten to 14 hours.

At the end of the day, you and your fellow crew members will take a courtesy bus to your hotel for the night. Your airline pays for your lodging on these **layovers**, but you are responsible for food and beverages as well as tips for the bus drivers who handle your bags. Your layover can range from six to eight hours (barely enough time for a good night's sleep), to as long as 16 to 24 hours giving you time to tour the local area. Multi–day layovers are becoming scarce in these tight–money times. Most crews on layovers shorter than 24 hours are put up at a hotel near the airport.

The next morning, you will accompany the rest of the crew back to the airport to begin again. Today you are on a cross–country flight (**trans–con**) with a more elaborate service that will keep you busy the entire flight. During the in–flight movie, you may have a chance to grab a meal and chat with your passengers and crew, unlike yesterday's flight which afforded little time for talking with passengers. Tonight's layover is in San Francisco for 21 hours, so you'll have time to go out for dinner at Fisherman's Wharf with the crew before turning in for the night.

Calculate your pretax monthly pay by adding your base pay plus any overtime and per diem.

The next morning, you will work three legs on the way home to your domicile where you'll enjoy two days off before reporting for your next flight. Adding up the legs of your trip, you flew 6,000 miles, served

nine meals, been away from home for 60 hours, and accrued 15 flight hours plus 60 hours of per diem. Four more of these three–day trips, and you will have completed your **bid month**.

So how much would you earn in a month of five trips like this one? To get a rough idea, let's apply Northwest Airlines' 2002 entry–level pay rates to this kind of schedule. Your pretax earnings would total $2101.54, based on the following calculations:

Flight hours:
[5 trips] x [15 flight hours per trip]
= 75 flight hours

Overtime:
[75 flight hours] — [65 hour monthly guarantee]
= 10 overtime hours

Per diem:
[5 trips] x [60 hours away from home per trip]
= 300 hours per diem

Base rate	=$1,340.34
Overtime (10 hours X $20.62)	= $206.20
Per diem (300 hours X $1.85)	= $555.00
Total Pay	=**$2,101.54**

In addition, some airlines offer additional pay rates for working on holidays, birthdays, at night, on understaffed flights, with reserve status, on over–water flights, as the "lead" flight attendant (also known as "A" flight attendant, number one, service manager, or purser), and for speaking a foreign language. A flight attendant will be paid a contractual dollar amount or an hourly flight–time rate for the accumulated number of hours spent completing required emergency and services training and for attending compulsory meetings. These rates of pay, in addition to periodic raises, vary from airline to airline. Your first salary increase usually comes after six to 12 months of active service.

Rather than use flight hours as the basis of your pay several airlines use the concept of a "trip," which consists of 243 miles. You are paid for the number of trips you complete in a month. For example, a 1,000-mile flight from Dallas to Denver would be worth four trips. Looking at Southwest Airlines' rate of pay, you would receive $58.68 for this one flight leg ($14.67 per trip times 4 trips = $58.68).

Especially during peak travel times or crew shortages, most airlines give flight attendants the option of picking up additional trips to earn additional overtime salary. Some airlines allow you to schedule yourself to work every day of the month for a lot of overtime — provided you satisfy and maintain proper legal rest as dictated by the FAA and your own work contract. Some airlines will even give you the option of dropping or trading away some or all of your flights in a month so that you would not have to report to work at all that month. Of course, your salary is determined by your flight hours, so the more or less you fly, the more or less you earn.

Most airlines also prefer to hire from within to fill openings for in–flight supervisors, trainers, and instructors. In addition, if you have the required education or training, it is possible to move on to become a pilot or enter the corporate structure.

✈ **Chapter 19**

YOUR FUTURE IN THE SKIES

You will never forget your experiences as a flight attendant, the places you see, or the people you meet.

The job of airline flight attendant can be the most interesting and challenging job you ever experience. If at first you don't succeed in landing the position, keep trying, because persistence pays off in this field. Some applicants may opt to start in another job with an airline — the so-called "ground" jobs — and transfer to a flight attendant position when one becomes available. Ground jobs include ticket agent, customer service agent, reservations agent, office staff, skycap, sales, and baggage handler, to name just a few. After several years of flying, some flight attendants opt to transfer into a managerial or supervisory position within their airline.

Whether you are a flight attendant for a few years or make it a career, you'll never forget the experiences you will have, the places you will see, or the people you will meet. You will have the opportunity, means, and time off to travel the world, continue your education, pursue a second career of interest, or just spend some quality time with your family and friends.

After nearly three decades of flying, I consider my job as a flight attendant to have been the best choice I ever made. It opened up opportunities I never dreamt existed. I'm looking forward to another two decades in the industry. Perhaps we'll have the opportunity to work together on a flight, and I can listen to all the exciting experiences you have enjoyed in your new flight attendant career.

✈ Chapter 20
AVIATION LINGO

You will greatly enhance your chances of getting hired and succeeding as a flight attendant if you know the airline industry's unique language. As suggested earlier, learn the terms in this chapter before your job interview and refresh your memory of them before you start your training.

Arm — The act of positioning an emergency slide or exit in the emergency–ready mode.

Base station — Stations where flight attendants are based. Also called a domicile or crew base.

Bidding — The process of selecting, in order of preference, a flight schedule from a master list or "bid package." The actual schedule is then determined in order of seniority.

Block to block — The period of time that starts when an aircraft leaves the airport gate to when it arrives at the next airport gate. Also known as "block hours."

Bulkhead — A wall separating cabins in an aircraft.

Business class — Mid–range cabin seats priced between coach and first class.

Cabin — The interior of an aircraft, where passengers are seated.

Charter flight — A unscheduled flight that may operate over regularly serviced routes, or over routes chosen by the booking party's needs.

Check–in time — The time at which a flight attendant is scheduled to arrive at the airport for duty.

Coach — The rear–most passenger section of the cabin. Also known as tourist class or economy.

Cockpit — The pilots' compartment in the front of the aircraft, also known as the "flight deck." During a flight, access is restricted to only active crew and FAA representatives.

Contract — A collectively negotiated working agreement between an airline and the members of a labor organization (union), which specifies hours of service, pay rates, working conditions, and other details of employment.

Corporate Contract Flight Attendant — A freelance flight attendant who contracts to work on corporate or private jets for a particular flight or period of time. Paid a daily rate plus expenses.

Corporate Full–Time Flight Attendant — A flight attendant employed full time by a corporation or private aircraft owner. Paid full salary and benefits.

CPR — Cardiopulmonary resuscitation, an emergency life support procedure that consists of the recognition and treatment of the absence of breathing and circulation.

CRAF — Civil Reserve Air Fleet. Military usage of commercial aircraft for transport of personnel.

Crew kit — Suitcase or bag flight attendants and pilots use for personal items.

Crew scheduling — Crew planning and scheduling office for an airline. Trades and changes in flight schedules are handled by crew scheduling.

Deadhead — To travel on company business in a non–working capacity. You may ride as a passenger to get to your flight assignment as part of your trip pairing. Not to be confused with fans of the Grateful Dead rock band

Domicile — A station at which flight attendants are based. Also called "base station."

Engineer — The pilot who is third in command. She maintains the electrical and mechanical systems of the aircraft. Some do not have an engineer.

EPM — *Emergency Procedures Manual* issued by airlines to flight attendants during training. The FAA requires all flight attendants to always carry the EPM when on duty.

ETA — Estimated time of arrival.

ETD — Estimated time of departure.

Evacuation — The procedure of getting passengers off an aircraft in the timeliest manner possible during an emergency.

Photograph of three early flight attendants reprinted by permission of Helen McLaughlin. Copyright 1994. All rights reserved.

Extra section — An additional flight added to a scheduled route in order to accommodate additional passengers.

FAA — Federal Aviation Administration.

FAR — Federal Aviation Regulation.

Ferry flight — Delivery of an aircraft to a destination without any passengers. Flight attendants may or may not accompany the aircraft.

First class — The premier class of service, usually in the front section of the airplane's cabin.

First officer — The second–in–command pilot on a flight.

Flight attendant — You, in a few months if all goes well. Also known as purser, cabin attendant, steward or stewardess, air hostess or host, or crew member. Attends to the safety and comfort of the passengers. Be sure to read the previous chapters in this book to fully understand the scope of the flight attendant's duties.

Flight pairings — Sequence of flights which make up each "trip."

Fractional Jet — A corporate jet shared by a few companies or individuals with each owning a *fraction* of the aircraft use each month.

Fuselage — The main body of the aircraft, excluding wings, tail, and engines.

Galley — The area on the aircraft where food is stored and prepared.

Gate — Passenger boarding area at an airport.

Hold a line — To work a scheduled sequence of flight pairings. See page 60.

Holding — The time during which an airplane waits to be cleared to land. Can also include holding time spent with passengers awaiting departure in a delayed situation.

Jetway — An enclosed passageway through which passengers move from airport to aircraft.

Job sharing — Splitting a bid month schedule with another flight attendant.

Jump seat — A fold–down seat for use by working flight attendants during taxi, takeoff, and turbulence.

Layover — A scheduled rest period away from the flight attendant's domicile while on a trip.

Leg — A portion of a flight trip. For example, flying from New York to Los Angeles would be one leg of a flight.

Legal rest — The minimum rest time required between or after flight time. The FAA establishes some legal rest requirements while the flight attendants' contract with the airlines sets others.

Legalities — Those scheduling rules and work provisions set by a negotiated contract agreement between the airline and flight attendants.

Line of time — A monthly sequence of flight pairings.

Non–routine — Not part of a regular schedule.

Off–line city — A city to which a particular airline does not fly.

Pass — Airline ticket used by an airline employee, eligible family member, or other eligible individual, that allows travel on a space–available basis for a nominal service charge. Depending on the airline, there may be a limit on the number of passes issued each year.

Per diem — Daily allowance for reimbursement of out of pocket expenses. Latin for "by the day."

Preflight — The act of checking emergency equipment and supplies on an aircraft prior to passenger boarding.

Ramp — The cement area adjacent to the terminal used for aircraft parking, loading, and unloading.

Reserve — An on–call flight attendant with no regular schedule.

Reserve line of time — Monthly schedule for flight attendants on reserve. May show scheduled days off.

Seniority — A flight attendant's precedence over others of the same rank by reason of a longer span of service. Seniority cannot be transferred between airlines. If a flight attendant moves from one airline to another, she loses all her seniority.

Special assignment — Assigned work that requires removing a flight attendant from a flight schedule. Instructing, promotions, and union business are examples of special assignments.

Standby — A flight attendant on reserve who is required to wait either at home or at the airport for an immediate flight assignment. Also, a passenger who has no reservation but is waiting for an open seat.

Taxi — Aircraft movement while on the ground.

Trans–con — A transcontinental, cross country, or coast–to–coast flight.

Turbulence — Irregular movement of the aircraft caused by changes in atmospheric air currents.

Turnaround flight — Any flight pairing that originates from and returns to the same city on the same day.

Z time — Mean solar time for the meridian at Greenwich, England, which is used as a basis for calculating time throughout most of the world. Also called "Greenwich mean time."

✈ **Chapter 21**
COMMON AIRPORT CODES

As explained earlier, flight attendants must learn these airport codes. These codes are also used throughout Chapter 25. You can find current airport codes for 9,000 airports worldwide online at http://www.airportcitycodes.com.

ABE	Allentown, PA
ABQ	Albuquerque, NM
ACY	Atlantic City, NJ
ALB	Albany, NY
ANC	Anchorage, AK
AOO	Altoona, PA
ATL	Atlanta, GA
ATW	Appleton, WI
AUS	Austin, TX
BDL	Hartford, CT
BGM	Binghamton, NY
BGR	Bangor, ME
BIL	Billings, MT
BNA	Nashville, TN
BOI	Boise, ID
BOS	Boston, MA
BUF	Buffalo, NY
BUR	Burbank, CA
BWI	Baltimore, MD
CAE	Columbia, SC
CHS	Charleston, SC
CKB	Clarksburg, WV
CLE	Cleveland, OH
CLT	Charlotte, NC
CMH	Columbus, OH
CPR	Casper, WY
CVG	Cincinnati, OH
DAL	Dallas, TX — Love Field
DAY	Dayton, OH
DCA	Washington, DC — Reagan National

DEN	Denver, CO
DFW	Dallas/Ft. Worth, TX
DSM	Des Moines, IA
DTW	Detroit, MI
DUJ	Dubois, PA
EEN	Keene, NH
ELP	El Paso, TX
EWN	New Bern, NC
EWR	Newark, NJ
FAR	Fargo, ND
FAT	Fresno, CA
FLL	Ft. Lauderdale, FL
FLO	Florence, SC
FNT	Flint, MI
FSD	Sioux Falls, SD
FWA	Ft. Wayne, IN
GEG	Spokane, WA
GJT	Grand Junction, CO
GON	New London, CT
GSP	Greenville/Spartanburg, SC
HNL	Honolulu, HI
HON	Huron, SD
HOU	Houston, TX — Hobby
IAD	Washington, DC — Dulles
IAH	Houston, TX — Intercont
ICT	Wichita, KS
IND	Indianapolis, IN
IPT	Williamsport, PA
JAN	Jackson, MS
JAX	Jacksonville, FL
JFK	New York, NY — JFK
JST	Johnstown, PA
LAN	Lansing, MI
LAS	Las Vegas, NV
LAX	Los Angeles, CA
LEX	Lexington, KY
LGA	New York, NY — La Guardia
LGB	Long Beach, CA
LGW	London, England — Gatwick

Common Airport Codes   75

LHR	London, England — Heathrow
LNS	Lancaster,PA
LYH	Lynchburg, VA
MAF	Midland, TX
MCI	Kansas City, MO
MCN	Macon, GA
MCO	Orlando, FL
MDT	Middletown, PA
MDW	Chicago, IL — Midway
MEM	Memphis, TN
MHT	Manchester, NH
MIA	Miami, FL
MKE	Milwaukee, WI
MOT	Minot, ND
MQT	Marquette, MI
MSN	Madison, WI
MSP	Minneapolis/St. Paul, MN
MSY	New Orleans, LA
OAK	Oakland, CA
OKC	Oklahoma City, OK
OMA	Omaha, NE
ONT	Ontario, CA
ORD	Chicago, IL — O'Hare
ORF	Norfolk, VA
ORH	Worcester, MA
PBI	West Palm Beach, FL
PDX	Portland, OR
PHF	Hampton, VA
PHL	Philadelphia, PA — Philadelphia International
PHX	Phoenix, AZ
PIT	Pittsburgh, PA
PNE	Philadelphia, PA — North Philadelphia Airport
PSP	Palm Springs, CA
PVD	Providence, RI
PWM	Portland, ME
RDD	Redding, CA
RDU	Raleigh/Durham, NC
RIC	Richmond, VA

RNO	Reno, NV
ROC	Rochester, NY
SAN	San Diego, CA
SAT	San Antonio, TX
SAV	Savannah, GA
SBY	Salisbury, MD
SDF	Louisville, KY
SCE	State College, PA
SEA	Seattle, WA
SFO	San Francisco, CA
SJC	San Jose, CA
SJU	San Juan, PR
SLC	Salt Lake City, UT
SLO	Salem, IL — Salem/Leckrone
SMF	Sacramento, CA
SNA	Orange County, CA
SPW	Spencer, IA
STL	St. Louis, MO
STT	St. Thomas, VI
STX	St. Croix, VI
SYR	Syracuse, NY
TPA	Tampa, FL
TUS	Tucson, AZ
YNG	Youngstown, OH

✈ Chapter 22
CANADIAN CITY CODES

As explained earlier, flight attendants must learn these codes. These codes are also used throughout Chapter 25.

YAM	Sault Ste. Marie, Ontario
YBA	Banff, Alberta
YDA	Dawson, Yukon Territory
YEA	Edmonton, Alberta
YHG	Charlottetown, Newfoundland
YHM	Hamilton, Ontario
YHZ	Halifax, Nova Scotia
YMX	Montreal, Quebec — Mirabel
YOW	Ottawa, Ontario
YPR	Prince Rupert, British Columbia
YQB	Quebec, Quebec
YQG	Windsor, Ontario
YQI	Yarmouth, Nova Scotia
YQM	Moncton, New Brunswick
YQR	Regina, Saskatchewan
YQT	Thunder Bay, Ontario
YQY	Sydney, Nova Scotia
YSB	Sudbury, Ontario
YTH	Thompson, Manitoba
YTS	Timmins, Ontario
YTZ	Toronto, Ontario — Toronto Island
YUL	Montreal, Quebec — Dorval
YVR	Vancouver, British Columbia
YWG	Winnipeg, Manitoba
YWS	Whistler, British Columbia
YXE	Saskatoon, Saskatchewan
YXU	London, Ontario
YXY	Whitehorse, Yukon
YYC	Calgary, Alberta
YYJ	Victoria, British Columbia
YYQ	Churchill, Manitoba
YYT	St. Johns, Newfoundland
YYZ	Toronto, Ontario — Pearson
YZF	Yellowknife, Northwest Territory

✈ **Chapter 23**
HOW TO APPLY

Chapter 25 consists of a directory of U.S. and Canadian airlines that gives the address for each airline's personnel or human resources office, or Flight Attendant Recruiting Office. This is the office to which you should write to obtain an application form if any is required. Some airlines will also list a job hotline, email address, or fax number where you should send your resume. A corporate website address, when available, is also listed.

After carefully reading each airline's synopsis and checking its requirements against your qualifications, select airlines whose eligibility benefits most fit your preferences. Write to the office listed for each airline you have chosen and request an application. You might use the following sample letter format as a guide, substituting the name of the airline to which you are applying for "[Airline]." Be sure to sign your letter before you send it.

Your home address
City, State Zip Code
Date

[Airline]
Address
City, State Zip Code

Dear Hiring Manager:

Having reviewed the qualifications for flight attendants with [Airline] described in the Flight Attendant Job Finder & Career Guide, I believe I would be a excellent candidate for the position, and an asset to your company.

Please mail to me a flight attendant job application which I will complete and return to you. Please also include any additional information about [airline] that would be relevant.

Thank you for your time and assistance.

Sincerely,

[Sign and type your name]

✈ Chapter 24
FINAL NOTES BEFORE TAKEOFF

I hope this guide will prove to be your greatest asset in landing your career in the skies. I wish you the best of success in acquiring the position and hope all your flights are full of interesting, but calm, passengers. Please write to me if I may be of any further assistance, or to pass on your comments and suggestions for possible inclusion in the next edition of the *Flight Attendant Job Finder & Career Guide.* I would really love to hear your stories! Please write to me at:

Tim Kirkwood
P.O. Box 6455
Delray Beach, FL 33482–6455

Or send me an email at: **crew4jets@aol.com**

I invite you to visit the **Aviation Employment Placement Service**'s Internet website for up–to–date job listings and interview dates, as well as aviation news and information. Simply enter this URL address in your web browser:

http://www.aeps.com

An excellent website for future and current flight attendants to visit is the online magazine, ***AviationCareer.net.*** This site has articles and first-hand accounts from flight attendants, as well as career advice. The site's searchable archive includes valuable articles. Visit the site at:

http://www.AviationCareer.net

✈ Chapter 25
THE AIRLINE LISTINGS

This chapter presents the key details about each U.S. and Canadian airline to help you decide which airlines would be best for you. Airlines appear in alphabetical order, starting with the U.S. airlines and then the Canadian. Information that is standard among all the airlines was proffered in Chapter 4, "Minimum Requirements for the Job," and is not repeated in these listings. The requirements discussed in Chapter 4 were:

✈ English language requirement;

✈ Pre–employment drug and alcohol test;

✈ Pre–employment physical;

✈ Weight in proportion to height;

✈ High School diploma or G.E.D.; and

✈ History of public contact work.

This chapter presents the information described in the paragraphs that follow for each U.S. and Canadian airline and each airline's requirements for flight attendants. When the listing for an airline notes that the requirement for a particular item is "pending" or "not available," that information simply was not available at the time this book went to press. Since it will be included on an upcoming free update sheet, be sure to check the latest update sheet for this book every few weeks. See page 167 for details on how to obtain the most recent free update sheet.

Type of airline: Indicates if the airline is a scheduled or charter carrier, or in some instances, a little of both. Chapter 10 beginning on page 27 explains the different types of airlines.

Resume required: Many airlines require you to submit your resume, with or without a cover letter. Even if a cover letter is not required, you would be prudent to include one with your resume so you can specify the position for which you are applying and highlight those items in your resume that make you a strong candidate for the job. Use your cover letter and resume to really sell yourself to the airline. Others require both a resume and an application form. Still others may require that you complete an application form or apply via their websites.

SASE required with application: Does the airline require you to send a self–addressed, stamped envelope with your application or application request? This is generally a number 10 business letter–size envelope. You will address the envelope to yourself, and affix sufficient postage. Include this in the envelope with your application and resume.

Application retained: This number indicates how long the airline will retain your application in its files. Once this period of time has passed, you can reapply to an airline.

Application fee: Some airlines charge a fee to process your application. Be sure to include a check or money order with your application.

Interviews/type: This indicates the usual number of interviews you will need to attend, and the type of interviews the airline uses. See Chapter 14 beginning on page 42 for more information on these different types of interviews.

Airline pays transportation to interview: Some airlines provide job candidates a "space–available pass" to attend an interview not in their local area. "On–line only" means the pass gets you from the city closest to you that the airline serves. It's your responsibility to get yourself to that departure city at your own expense.

Height: Minimum and maximum height requirements to work for the airline. Many airlines will have no set requirements, and some require a "reach test" to see if you can touch a specified height.

Minimum age: The youngest you can be to work for this airline. There is no maximum age limit. Local laws that govern the handling of liquor usually determine the minimum age.

Language(s) preferred: These are the languages that an airline would prefer that you speak in addition to English. For example, an airline that flies to South

America would prefer Spanish and Portuguese but would have little need for flight attendants who speak Swedish or Arabic.

Base pay/minimum hours: "Base pay" is the monthly pay rate, before overtime and any additional rates of pay. "Minimum hours" are the number of flight hours required to work to receive your base pay. Some airlines list their salaries by the hour, while others indicate theirs by the month or year. The hourly rate may be determined by dividing the monthly rate by the minimum flight hours per month. For example, a monthly salary of $1,050 divided by 75 hours equals $14 per hour.

Overtime rate: The salary overtime rate kicks in when you exceed the monthly minimum hours. When no overtime rate is listed, the airline does not have an overtime rate; the regular hourly rate would apply to any overtime served.

Per Diem: Hourly or daily allowance for reimbursement of out–of–pocket expenses.

Uniform costs: Average cost of an initial uniform. Some airlines will split the cost of the first uniform or

Keep up to date!

Updates of the airline listings in this chapter are available for free on the Internet. See page 167 for details.

charge nothing at all. Most will allow payroll deduction of uniform costs. The amount given here is the flight attendant's share of his uniform costs.

Training length/location: This item tells how long the airline's flight attendant training program lasts, and identifies the city or cities where it is held. Use the airport codes listed in Chapters 21 and 22 to identify the cities.

Training cost: The cost to the employee to complete training, excluding housing and food.

Salary earned while in training: The salary you will earn while in the airline's flight attendant training program. Some airlines will reimburse the trainee only after she successfully completes the training program.

Company-paid housing provided: If the training is not in your local area, some airlines provide prepaid housing for its flight attendant trainees.

Domiciles: The cities where an airline's flight attendant work force is based. Not all domiciles will be available after you complete training. Several airlines will indicate one domicile in New York City, with flights operating out of the La Guardia (LGA), John F. Kennedy (JFK), and Newark, NJ (EWR) airports. Use the airport codes listed in Chapters 21 and 22 to identify the cities.

Flight Attendant Union: The union, if any, that represents the flight attendants at this airline.

Application address: At the end of each airline's listing is the address to which you send your request for an application, or if only a resume is required, to which you send your resume and cover letter.

Phone number: This will be the airline's job hotline number, or a fax number to send your resume to the Human Resources or In-Flight Department.

Instructions: Any additional directions for applying, including using the company website to apply.

Website: The URL, or address, of the airline's website. If the site's home page is listed, you will need to navigate your way to the website's employment page.

✈ U.S. AIRLINES

Remember that an American airline can hire only U.S. citizens and resident aliens who possess a valid work permit.

Pay scales are in U.S. dollars unless specified otherwise.

Be sure to read the previous chapters before examining these airline listings.

See page 167 to learn how to receive free updates to these listings.

✈ AIR TRANSPORT INTERNATIONAL

Airline type: **Charter**

Resume required: **Yes, with cover letter**

SASE required with application: **No**

Application retained: **12 months**

Application fee: **None**

Interviews/type: **One / individual**

Airline pays transportation to interview: **No**

Height: **None**   Minimum age: **20**

Language(s) preferred: **None**

Base pay/minimum hours: **$1,828 per 28–day bid month**

Overtime rate: **$22/hour**

Per diem: **$1.50/hour domestic, $2/hour international**

Uniform costs: **$400**

Training length/location: **21 days / DAY**

Training cost: **None**

Salary during training: **$500/month**

Company–paid housing provided: **Yes**

Domiciles: **Various**

Flight attendant union: **None**

Air Transport International

2800 Cantrell Road

Suite 400

Little Rock, AR 72202-2049

501/603–2030

Instructions: No unsolicited resumes

Website: http://www.airtransport.cc/

✈ AIR WISCONSIN

Airline type: **Scheduled**

Resume required: **No**

SASE required with application: **Yes**

Application retained: **12 months**

Application fee: None

Interviews/type: **Two / group, one–on–one**

Airline pays transportation to interview: **On–line**

Height: **None**   Minimum age: **19**

Language(s) preferred: **None**

Base pay/minimum hours: **$16.34 per hour / 70 hours**

Overtime rate: **$16.34/hour**

Per diem: **$1.55/hour**

Uniform costs: **$525 to $575**

Training length/location: **6 weeks / DEN**

Training cost: **None**

Salary during training: **$25/day**

Company–paid housing provided: **Yes**

Domiciles: **ATW DEN ORD**

Flight attendant union: **Association of Flight Attendants**

Air Wisconsin

Attn: Human Resources

W6390 Challenger Drive

Appleton, WI 54915–9120

888/354–4505

Instructions: Flight attendant applications are always accepted. Recruiting sessions are by invitation only; invitations are sent to qualified applicants. Applicants must confirm that they will be attending the recruiting session.

Website: www.airwis.com

✈ AIRTRAN AIRWAYS

Airline type: **Scheduled**

Resume required: **Yes**

SASE required with application: **No**

Application retained: **1 month**

Application fee: **$25**

Interviews/type: **Three / open house, group, individual**

Airline pays transportation to interview: **Yes**

Height: **5'2" to 6'2"**   Minimum age: **19**

Language(s) preferred: **Bilingual a plus**

Base pay/minimum hours: **$18.56 per hour / 70 hours**

Overtime rate: **None**

Per diem: **$1.25/hour**

Uniform costs: **$500**

Training length/location: **20 days / ATW**

Training cost: **None**

Salary during training: **Bonus after completion**

Company–paid housing provided: **Out–of–town trainees only**

Domiciles: **ATW**

Flight attendant union: **Association of Flight Attendants**

AirTran Airways
Attn: Human Resources
9955 AirTran Blvd.
Orlando, FL 32827–5385
888/833–6706

Instructions: Open house by invitation only.

Website: www.airtran.com/aboutus/employ/index.jsp

✈ ALASKA AIRLINES

Airline type: **Scheduled**
Resume required: **No**
SASE required with application: **No**
Application retained: **12 months**
Application fee: **None**
Interviews/type: **Three / group, group, private**
Airline pays transportation to interview: **No**
Height: **80" reach**   Minimum age: **21**
Language(s) preferred: **None**
Base pay/minimum hours: **$15.27 per trip (243 miles)**
Overtime rate: **Varies**
Per diem: **$2/hour**
Uniform costs: **$700**
Training length/location: **5 weeks / SEA**
Training cost: **None**
Salary during training: **$20/hour**
Company–paid housing provided: **Non–Seattle residents only**
Domiciles: **SEA ANC LAX PDX**
Flight attendant union: **Association of Flight Attendants**

Alaska Airlines
Attn: Flight Attendant Hiring
P.O. Box 68900
Seattle, WA 98168–0900
206/433–3230

Website: www.alaskaair.com

✈ ALLEGHENY AIRLINES / USAIRWAYS EXPRESS

Airline type: **Scheduled**

Resume required: **Yes**

SASE required with application: **No**

Application retained: **12 months**

Application fee: **None**

Interviews/type: **Two / group, panel**

Airline pays transportation to interview: **On–line**

Height: **6'1" maximum**   Minimum age: **19**

Language(s) preferred: **None**

Base pay/minimum hours: **$14.18 per hour / 70 hours**

Overtime rate: **$14.18/hour**

Per diem: **$1.35/hour**

Uniform costs: **$650**

Training length/location: **4 weeks / MDT**

Training cost: **None**

Salary during training: **$992 after successful completion**

Company–paid housing provided: **Yes**

Domiciles: **MDT SYR BGM ABE SCE**

Flight attendant union: **Association of Flight Attendants**

Allegheny Airlines
Attn: Human Resources
1000 Rosedale Avenue
Middletown, PA 17057–0432
Fax: 717/948–5548

Website: www.alleghenyairlines.com

✈ ALLEGIANT AIR

Airline type: **Scheduled**
Resume required: **Yes**
SASE required with application: **No**
Application retained: **6 months**
Application fee: **None**
Interviews/type: **Three / group, panel, individual**
Airline pays transportation to interview: **No**
Height: **5'2" minimum**   Minimum age: **21**
Language(s) preferred: **Spanish**
Base pay/minimum hours: **$18,000/year**
Overtime rate: **None**
Per diem: **$1/hour**
Uniform costs: **$800**
Training length/location: **3 weeks / FAT**
Training cost: **None**
Salary during training: **Per diem**
Company–paid housing provided: **No**
Domiciles: **FAT IFP**
Flight attendant union: **None**

Allegiant Air
4955 E. Andersen Avenue
Suite 120
Fresno, CA 93727–1545
559/454–7708
Website: www.allegiantair.com

✈ ALOHA AIRLINES

Airline type: **Scheduled**
Resume required: **No**
SASE required with application: **No**
Application retained: **6 months**
Application fee: **None**
Interviews/type: **Two / group, private**
Airline pays transportation to interview: **No**
Height: **75" reach**   Minimum age: **18**
Language(s) preferred: **None**
Base pay/minimum hours: **$17.64 per hour / 75 hours**
Overtime rate: **$17.64/hour**
Per diem: **$1.75/hour**
Uniform costs: **$300**
Training length/location: **4 weeks / HNL**
Training cost: **None**
Salary during training: **None**
Company–paid housing provided: **No**
Domiciles: **HNL**
Flight attendant union: **Association of Flight Attendants**

Aloha Airlines
Attn: Staffing Dept.
P.O. Box 30028
Honolulu, HI 96820–0028
808/836–4109

Website: www.alohaair.com

✈ ALOHA ISLAND AIR

Airline type: **Scheduled**

Resume required: **No**

SASE required with application: **No**

Application retained: **3 months**

Application fee: **None**

Interviews/type: **Two / group, private**

Airline pays transportation to interview: **No**

Height: **5' to 6'**   Minimum age: **18**

Language(s) preferred: **Japanese**

Base pay/minimum hours: **Varies**

Overtime rate: **Varies**

Per diem: **None**

Uniform costs: **None**

Training length/location: **3 weeks / HNL**

Training cost: **None**

Salary during training: **Yes**

Company–paid housing provided: **No**

Domiciles: **HNL**

Flight attendant union: **None**

Aloha Island Air
99 Kapalulu Place
Honolulu, HI 96819–1843

Instructions: Flight Attendants are cross–utilized as customer service agents. Applications accepted via open house only.

Website: http://www.islandair.com

✈ AMERICA WEST AIRLINES

Airline type: **Scheduled**

Resume required: **No**

SASE required with application: **No**

Application retained: **6 months**

Application fee: **None**

Interviews/type: **Three / group, private, private**

Airline pays transportation to interview: **On–line**

Height: **None**   Minimum age: **20**

Language(s) preferred: **Spanish**

Base pay/minimum hours: **$12,944 per year / 70 hours**

Overtime rate: **$15.41/hour**

Per diem: **$1.30/hour**

Uniform costs: **$500**

Training length/location: **7 weeks / Tempe**

Training cost: **None**

Salary during training: **$20/day**

Company–paid housing provided: **No**

Domiciles: **PHX plus satellites @ LAS**

Flight attendant union: **Association of Flight Attendants**

America West Airlines

Attn: Employment Dept.

4000 E. Sky Harbor Blvd.

Phoenix, AZ 85034–3802

877/AWA–4JOB

Instructions: Passport required.
Email: employment@americawest.com

Website: www.americawest.com

✈ AMERICAN AIRLINES

Airline type: **Scheduled**

Resume required: **No**

SASE required with application: **No**

Application retained: **12 months**

Application fee: **None**

Interviews/type: **One / group**

Airline pays transportation to interview: **Yes**

Height: **5'1" to 6'**   Minimum age: **20**

Language(s) preferred: **Japanese, Swedish, Spanish, French, Portuguese, German, Italian, Dutch, and other languages**

Base pay/minimum hours: **$21.61 per hour / 67 hours**

Overtime rate: **$24.85/hour**

Per diem: **$1.85/hour domestic, $2.05/hour international**

Uniform costs: **$800 to $1000**

Training length/location: **6½ weeks / DFW**

Training cost: **None**

Salary during training: **None**

Company–paid housing provided: **Yes**

Domiciles: **NYC SFO LAX MIA ORD DCA DFW STL BOS**

Flight attendant union: **Association of Professional Flight Attendants**

American Airlines
P.O. Box 619410
Mail Drop 4125
Dallas–Ft. Worth, TX 75261–9410
Website: www.aa.com

✈ AMERICAN EAGLE AIRLINES

Airline type: **Scheduled**

Resume required: **No**

SASE required with application: **Yes**

Application retained: **24 months**

Application fee: **None**

Interviews/type: **Two / group, one–on–one**

Airline pays transportation to interview: **Yes**

Height: **5' to 5'10"**   Minimum age: **19**

Language(s) preferred: **None**

Base pay/minimum hours: **$17.67 per hour / 75 hours**

Overtime rate: **$17.67/hour**

Per diem: **$1.30/hour**

Uniform costs: **$750 to $800**

Training length/location: **3½ weeks / DFW**

Training cost: **None**

Salary during training: **None**

Company–paid housing provided: **Yes**

Domiciles: **ORD DFW LAX SJU MIA BOS JFK**

Flight attendant union: **Association of Flight Attendants**

American Eagle Airlines Inc.

Mail Drop 4127

P.O. Box 619415

Dallas–Ft. Worth Airport, TX 75261–9415

Website: http:// www.americaneaglecareers.com/

✈ AMERICAN TRANS AIR

Airline type: **Both**

Resume required: **No**

SASE required with application: **No**

Application retained: **6 months**

Application fee: **None**

Interviews/type: **Two / group, individual**

Airline pays transportation to interview: **No**

Height: **None** Minimum age: **20**

Language(s) preferred: **German, French, Portuguese, Spanish**

Base pay/minimum hours: **$18.19 per hour / 75 hours**

Overtime rate: **Time–and–a–half over 82 hours**

Per diem: **$1/hour turnarounds, $1.50/hour domestic, $2/hour international**

Uniform costs: **$400 to $600**

Training length/location: **5 weeks / IND**

Training cost: **None**

Salary during training: **Meal allowance**

Company–paid housing provided: **Yes**

Domiciles: **IND ORD LGA SFO LAX**

Flight attendant union: **Association of Flight Attendants**

American Trans Air
Attn: Flight Attendant/Corporate Recruiter
P.O. Box 51609
Indianapolis, IN 46251–0609
Website: www.ata.com

✈ ATLANTIC COAST AIRLINES

Airline type: **Scheduled**

Resume required: **No**

SASE required with application: **No**

Application retained: **12 months**

Application fee: **None**

Interviews/type: **Two / group, one–on–one**

Airline pays transportation to interview: **On–line only**

Height: **None**   Minimum age: **18**

Language(s) preferred: **None**

Base pay/minimum hours: **$15.23 per hour / 75 hours**

Overtime rate: **None**

Per diem: **$1.55/hour**

Uniform costs: **$450**

Training length/location: **4 weeks (UA) 3 weeks (DL) / IAD**

Training cost: **None**

Salary during training: **$28/day**

Company–paid housing provided: **Out–of–town trainees only**

Domiciles: **IAD ORD BOS LGA**

Flight attendant union: **Association of Flight Attendants**

Atlantic Coast Airlines

Attn: Recruiting Department

515–A Shaw Road

Dulles, VA 20166–9402

Website: www.atlanticcoast.com

✈ ATLANTIC SOUTHEAST AIRLINES / DELTA CONNECTION

Airline type: **Scheduled**

Resume required: **Yes**

SASE required with application: **No**

Application retained: **12 months**

Application fee: **None**

Interviews/type: **Two / group, private**

Airline pays transportation to interview: **On–line only**

Height: **None**   Minimum age: **20**

Language(s) preferred: **None**

Base pay/minimum hours: **$15.35 per hour / 70 hours**

Overtime rate: **None**

Per diem: **$1.50/hour**

Uniform costs: **$500**

Training length/location: **4½ weeks / ATW**

Training cost: **None**

Salary during training: **$20/day**

Company–paid housing provided: **Out–of–town trainees only**

Domiciles: **ATW DFW**

Flight attendant union: **Association of Flight Attendants**

Atlantic Southeast Airlines

Attn: Flight Attendant Recruiter

100 Hartsfield Centre Parkway, Suite 300

Atlanta, GA 30354–1356

Fax: 404/209–0452

Instructions: Fax or mail your resume, or visit the website.

Website: www.flyasa.com

✈ CARIBBEAN STAR AIRLINE

Airline type: **Scheduled**

Resume required: **Yes**

SASE required with application: **No**

Application retained: **6 months**

Application fee: **None**

Interviews/type: **Two / group, individual**

Airline pays transportation to interview: **No**

Height: **None**   Minimum age: **19**

Language(s) preferred: **None**

Base pay/minimum hours: **$24,000 per year / 70
        hours**

Overtime rate: **None**

Per diem: **$36/day for overnight**

Uniform costs: **None**

Training length/location: **3 weeks / FLL**

Training cost: **None**

Salary during training: **$50/day**

Company–paid housing provided: **None**

Domiciles: **SJU**

Flight attendant union: **None**

Caribbean Star Airline, Inc.
**610 SW 34th Street, Suite 303
Ft. Lauderdale, FL 33315–3623
Fax: 954/359–7848**

Website: www.flycaribbeanstar.com

✈ CASINO EXPRESS AIRLINES

Airline type: **Both**

Resume required: **Yes**

SASE required with application: **Yes**

Application retained: **6 months**

Application fee: **None**

Interviews/type: **Two / group, individual**

Airline pays transportation to interview: **Sometimes**

Height: **None**   Minimum age: **21**

Language(s) preferred: **None**

Base pay/minimum hours: **$15.50 per hour / 60 hours**

Overtime rate: **$15.50/hour**

Per diem: **$1.25/hour**

Uniform costs: **None**

Training length/location: **2 weeks / EKO**

Training cost: **None**

Salary during training: **$46.50/day**

Company–paid housing provided: **Out–of–town trainees only**

Domiciles: **EKO MEM**

Flight attendant union: **None**

Casino Express Airlines
Attn: In–Flight Manager
976 Mountain City Highway
Elko, NV 89801–2728

✈ CCAIR

Airline type: **Scheduled**

Resume required: **Yes**

SASE required with application: **No**

Application retained: **12 months**

Application fee: **None**

Interviews/type: **Two / panel, private**

Airline pays transportation to interview: **On–line**

Height: **None**   Minimum age: **19**

Language(s) preferred: **None**

Base pay/minimum hours: **$15.07 per hour / 70 hours**

Overtime rate: **$15.07/hour**

Per diem: **$1.40/hour**

Uniform costs: **$350**

Training length/location: **2 weeks / CLT**

Training cost: **None**

Salary during training: **Half of guarantee**

Company–paid housing provided: **Out–of–town trainees only**

Domiciles: **CLT AGS OAJ TLH PGV**

Flight attendant union: **Association of Flight Attendants**

CCAir, Inc.
Flight Attendant Recruiting
4700 Yorkmont Road
Charlotte, NC 28208–7344
Website: www.ccairinc.com

✈ CHAMPION AIR

Airline type: **Charter**

Resume required: **No**

SASE required with application: **No**

Application retained: **6 months**

Application fee: **None**

Interviews/type: **Three / open house, group, one–on–one**

Airline pays transportation to interview: **No**

Height: **5'2" to 6'1"**   Minimum age: **19**

Language(s) preferred: **Spanish**

Base pay/minimum hours: **$16.31 per hour / 65 hours**

Overtime rate: **$16.31/hour**

Per diem: **$1.50/hour domestic, $2.10/hour international**

Uniform costs: **$400**

Training length/location: **4 weeks / MSP**

Training cost: **None**

Salary during training: **None**

Company–paid housing provided: **Yes**

Domiciles: **MSP DEN DTW DFW STL**

Flight attendant union: **None**

Champion Air

8009 34th Avenue South

Suite 700

Bloomington, MN 55425–1616

Instructions: Apply online via website, or email resume to employment@championair.com

Website: www.championair.com

✈ CHAUTAUQUA AIRLINES

Airline type: **Scheduled**

Resume required: **Yes**

SASE required with application: **No**

Application retained: **12 months**

Application fee: **None**

Interviews/type: **Two / group, individual**

Airline pays transportation to interview: **On–line USAirways**

Height: **None**   Minimum age: **19**

Language(s) preferred: **None**

Base pay/minimum hours: **$15.13 per hour / 75 hours**

Overtime rate: **None**

Per diem: **$1.35/hour**

Uniform costs: **$300**

Training length/location: **2½ weeks / IND**

Training cost: **None**

Salary during training: **Yes**

Company–paid housing provided: **Yes**

Domiciles: **PHL IND LGA CMH RIC BOS STL**

Flight attendant union: **International Brotherhood of Teamsters**

Chautauqua Airlines
Suite 160
2500 S. High School Road
Indianapolis, IN 46241–4941
Fax: 317/484–4747

Instructions: Apply via fax, mail, or online at the website.

Website: www.flychautauqua.com/

✈ CHICAGO EXPRESS AIRLINES / ATA CONNECTION

Airline type: **Scheduled**

Resume required: **Preferred**

SASE required with application: **No**

Application retained: **6 months**

Application fee: **None**

Interviews/type: **Varies by size**

Airline pays transportation to interview: **On-line only**

Height: **5'1" to 5'10"**   Minimum age: **19**

Language(s) preferred: **Spanish**

Base pay/minimum hours: **$16 per hour / 75 hours**

Overtime rate: **Time-and-a-half**

Per diem: **$25/day**

Uniform costs: **$600**

Training length/location: **4 weeks / MDW**

Training cost: **None**

Salary during training: **65 hours**

Company-paid housing provided: **Yes**

Domiciles: **MDW**

Flight attendant union: **None**

Chicago Express Airlines

Attn: Human Resources

5333 S. Laramie Avenue

Chicago, IL 60638-3035

Website: www.ata.com/prod_svcs/ ata_connex.html

✈ COLGAN AIR

Airline type: **Scheduled**

Resume required: **Yes**

SASE required with application: **No**

Application retained: **12 months**

Application fee: **None**

Interviews/type: **Two / group, individual**

Airline pays transportation to interview: **On–line**

Height: **None**   Minimum age: **18**

Language(s) preferred: **None**

Base pay/minimum hours: **$16 per hour / 75 hours**

Overtime rate: **None**

Per diem: **$1.10/hour**

Uniform costs: **$200**

Training length/location: **2 weeks / MNZ**

Training cost: **None**

Salary during training: **Yes, retroactively**

Company–paid housing provided: **Out–of–town trainees only**

Domiciles: **MNZ HTS HYA PVD**

Flight attendant union: **None**

Colgan Air, Inc.
Attn: Kim Jennings
10652 Wakeman Court, Suite 102
Manassas, VA 20110–2026
Fax: 703/393–9507

Instructions: Apply via email to kimjennings@colganair.com

Website: www.colganair.com/

✈ COMAIR / DELTA CONNECTION

Airline type: **Scheduled**

Resume required: **Yes**

SASE required with application: **No**

Application retained: **6 months**

Application fee: **None**

Interviews/type: **Two / phone screen, individual**

Airline pays transportation to interview: ~~**No**~~ *yes*

Height: **5'10" maximum**   Minimum age: **21**

Language(s) preferred: **French, Spanish**

Base pay/minimum hours: **~~$19.10~~ per hour / 78 hours**   *20.97*

Overtime rate: **$19.10/hour**

Per diem: **$~~1.30~~/hour** *1.75*

Uniform costs: **$600**

Training length/location: **4½ weeks / CVG**

Training cost: **None**

Salary during training: **$~~100/week~~** *none*

Company–paid housing provided: **Out–of–town trainees only** *yes*

Domiciles: **MCO CVG**

Flight attendant union: **International Brotherhood of Teamsters**

ComAir

Atten: Cindy Boone

P.O. Box 75352

Cincinnati, OH 45275–0352

859/767–1330

Instructions: Fax resume with 10–year work and school history to 859/767–2874

Website: www.fly-comair.com

✈ CONTINENTAL AIRLINES

Airline type: **Scheduled**

Resume required: **Yes**

SASE required with application: **No**

Application retained: **6 months**

Application fee: **None**

Interviews/type: **Two / one–on–one, panel**

Airline pays transportation to interview: **On–line**

Height: **5' minimum**   Minimum age: **20**

Language(s) preferred: **Italian, French, Portuguese, Russian, German, Spanish**

Base pay/minimum hours: **$23.15 per hour / 83 hours**

Overtime rate: **$23.15/hour**

Per diem: **$1.95/hour domestic, $2.50/hour international**

Uniform costs: **$720**

Training length/location: **6 weeks / IAH**

Training cost: **None**

Salary during training: **$105/week**

Company–paid housing provided: **Yes**

Domiciles: **CLE IAH EWR**

Flight attendant union: **International Association of Machinists**

Continental Airlines
Suite 410F HQSNR
1600 Smith Street
Houston, TX 77002–7362
800/444–8414 extension 69562#
Website: www.continental.com

✈ CONTINENTAL MICRONESIA

Airline type: **Scheduled**
Resume required: **Yes**
SASE required with application: **No**
Application retained: **6 months**
Application fee: **None**
Interviews/type: **Two or three / group, private**
Airline pays transportation to interview: **No**
Height: **5' to 6'**   Minimum age: **19**
Language(s) preferred: **Japanese, Chinese**
Base pay/minimum hours: **$16.50 per hour / 75 hours**
Overtime rate: **$21.50/hour**
Per diem: **$2.35/hour**
Uniform costs: **None**
Training length/location: **7 to 8 weeks / Guam**
Training cost: **None**
Salary during training: **None**
Company–paid housing provided: **No**
Domiciles: **Guam**
Flight attendant union: **International Association of Machinists**

Continental Micronesia
Personnel Department
P.O. Box 8778–N
Tamuning, GU 96928–1741

✈ DELTA AIR LINES

Airline type: **Scheduled**

Resume required: **Yes, only**

SASE required with application: **No**

Application retained: **12 months**

Application fee: **None**

Interviews/type: **Two / group, private**

Airline pays transportation to interview: **On–line**

Height: **None**   Minimum age: **20**

Language(s) preferred: **Czech, Greek, Dutch, Italian, Portuguese, Turkish, Japanese**

Base pay/minimum hours: **$3,126 per month / 80 hours**

Overtime rate: **None**

Per diem: **$2.25/hour domestic, $2.35/hour international**

Uniform costs: **$600**

Training length/location: **5 weeks / ATW**

Training cost: **None**

Salary during training: **None**

Company–paid housing provided: **Yes, for non–Atlanta residents**

Domiciles: **ATW ~~ORD~~ BOS SLC LAX MCO MIA NYC ~~SEA PDX MSY IAH~~ DFW CVG**

Flight attendant union: **None**

Delta Air Lines, Inc

Recruitment and Employment Office

P.O. Box 20530

Atlanta, GA 30320–2530

Instructions: Only accepts resumes and applications when opportunities are available. Visit the website for the latest flight attendant career information.

Website: www.delta.com

✈ EAGLE JET

Airline type: **Both**
Resume required: **Yes**
SASE required with application: **Yes**
Application retained: **12 months**
Application fee: **None**
Interviews/type: **Individual**
Airline pays transportation to interview: **No**
Height: **5'2" to 6'2"**   Minimum age: **21**
Language(s) preferred: **Japanese**
Base pay/minimum hours: **$11,400 per year / 160 duty hours**
Overtime rate: **$11.79/hour**
Per diem: **$1.50/hour for overnight**
Uniform costs: **None**
Training length/location: **2 weeks / LAS**
Training cost: **None**
Salary during training: **$500**
Company–paid housing provided: **No**
Domiciles: **LAS**
Flight attendant union: **None**

Eagle Jet
Atten: Chief Flight Attendant
275 E. Tropicana, Suite 100
Las Vegas, NV 89109–7360

✈ ERA AVIATION

Airline type: **Both**

Resume required: **Yes**

SASE required with application: **No**

Application retained: **2 months**

Application fee: **None**

Interviews/type: **Three / group, one–on–one, one–on–one**

Airline pays transportation to interview: **No**

Height: **None**   Minimum age: **21**

Language(s) preferred: **None**

Base pay/minimum hours: **$18,305 per year**

Overtime rate: **$19.60/hour**

Per diem: **$40/day**

Uniform costs: **$800**

Training length/location: **2 weeks / ANC**

Training cost: **None**

Salary during training: **Minimum wage**

Company–paid housing provided: **No**

Domiciles: **ANC**

Flight attendant union: **None**

ERA Aviation

Attn: Brenda Mahar

6160 Carl Brady Drive

Anchorage, AK 99502–1801

Fax: 907/266–8401

Instructions: Applications can be downloaded from the website and mailed or faxed.

Website: www.era–aviation.com

✈ EXPRESS JET

Airline type: **Scheduled**
Resume required: **Yes**
SASE required with application: **No**
Application retained: **6 months**
Application fee: **None**
Interviews/type: **Two / group, panel**
Airline pays transportation to interview: **Yes**
Height: **5' to 5'9"**   Minimum age: **20**
Language(s) preferred: **Spanish, French**
Base pay/minimum hours: **$16.28 per hour / 80 hours**   17.11
Overtime rate: **None**
Per diem: **$1.40/hour**
Uniform costs: **$750**
Training length/location: **5½ weeks / HOU**
Training cost: **None**
Salary during training: **$24/day**
Company–paid housing provided: **Yes**
Domiciles: **EWR CLE HOU**
Flight attendant union: **International Association of Machinists**

Express Jet
1600 Smith Street
Houston, TX 77002–7362
Fax: 281/553–4016

Instructions: Apply via website or fax resume.

Website: www.expressjetair.com/

✈ FALCON AIR EXPRESS

Airline type: **Charter**

Resume required: **Yes**

SASE required with application: **No**

Application retained: **6 months**

Application fee: **None**

Interviews/type: **Three / Open house, one–on–one, one–on–one**

Airline pays transportation to interview: **No**

Height: **5'2" to 6'**   Minimum age: **21**

Language(s) preferred: **French, French Creole, Spanish, Dutch**

Base pay/minimum hours: **$18 per hour / 65 hours**

Overtime rate: **$18/hour**

Per diem: **$36/day for overnight**

Uniform costs: **$500**

Training length/location: **4 weeks / MIA**

Training cost: **None**

Salary during training: **$36/day**

Company–paid housing provided: **No**

Domiciles: **MIA**

Flight attendant union: **None**

Falcon Air Express
Attn: In–Flight
9500 NW 41st Street
Miami, FL 33178–2304

Instructions: Be sure to have an application on file. Apply via website.

Website: www.falconairexpress.net

✈ FRONTIER AIRLINES

Airline type: **Scheduled**

Resume required: **Only at open house**

SASE required with application: **No**

Application retained: **6 months**

Application fee: **$15**

Interviews/type: **Three / group, one–on–one, final board**

Airline pays transportation to interview: **On–line**

Height: **5'1" to 6'4"**   Minimum age: **21**

Language(s) preferred: **None**

Base pay/minimum hours: **$1,500 per month / 85 hours**

Overtime rate: **Time–and–a–half**

Per diem: **$1.60/hour**

Uniform costs: **$350**

Training length/location: **5 weeks / DEN**

Training cost: **None**

Salary during training: **$1,500/month**

Company–paid housing provided: **No**

Domiciles: **DEN**

Flight attendant union: **None**

Frontier Airlines
Attn: In–Flight
7001 Tower Road
Denver, CO 80249–7312
Website: www.flyfrontier.com

✈ GREAT PLAINS AIRLINES

Airline type: **Both**

Resume required: **Yes**

SASE required with application: **No**

Application retained: **6 months**

Application fee: **None**

Interviews/type: **Three / group, individual, individual**

Airline pays transportation to interview: **On–line**

Height: **None**   Minimum age: **21**

Language(s) preferred: **None**

Base pay/minimum hours: **$15.50 per hour / 80 hours**

Overtime rate: **$15.50/hour**

Per diem: **$25/overnight**

Uniform costs: **$100**

Training length/location: **2 weeks / COU**

Training cost: **None**

Salary during training: **$15.50 per hour / 40 hours**

Company–paid housing provided: **Yes**

Domiciles: **TUL**

Flight attendant union: **None**

Great Plains Airlines
6501 East Apache Street
Tulsa, OK 74115–3639
Website: www.gpair.com

GULFSTREAM INTERNATIONAL / CONTINENTAL CONNECTION

Airline type: **Scheduled**

Resume required: **Yes**

SASE required with application: **No**

Application retained: **6 months**

Application fee: **None**

Interviews/type: **Two / open house, individual**

Airline pays transportation to interview: **No**

Height: **5'2" to 6'**   Minimum age: **19**

Language(s) preferred: **Spanish**

Base pay/minimum hours: **$16 per hour / 70 hours**

Overtime rate: **$16/hour**

Per diem: **$1.75/hour for overnight**

Uniform costs: **None**

Training length/location: **3 weeks / FLL**

Training cost: **None**

Salary during training: **$650 upon completion**

Company–paid housing provided: **No**

Domiciles: **FLL**

Flight attendant union: **None**

Gulfstream International / Continental Connection

1550 SW 43rd Street

Ft. Lauderdale, FL 33315–3546

Fax: 954/359–8036

Website: www.gulfstreamair.com

✈ HAWAIIAN AIRLINES

Airline type: **Scheduled**

Resume required: **Yes**

SASE required with application: **Yes**

Application retained: **6 months**

Application fee: **None**

Interviews/type: **Four to five / Varies**

Airline pays transportation to interview: **No**

Height: **5'2" to 6'**   Minimum age: **18**

Language(s) preferred: **Japanese, French, Tongan, Samoan, Tahitian**

Base pay/minimum hours: **$15.64 per hour / 75 hours**

Overtime rate: **$15.64/hour**

Per diem: **$1.40/hour inter–island, $1.80/hour international**

Uniform costs: **$800**

Training length/location: **6 weeks / HNL**

Training cost: **None**

Salary during training: **Per diem**

Company–paid housing provided: **No**

Domiciles: **LAX HNL**

Flight attendant union: **Association of Flight Attendants**

Hawaiian Airlines
Attn: Flight Attendant Recruitment
P.O. Box 30008
Honolulu, HI 96820–0008
Website: www.hawaiianair.com

✈ HORIZON AIR

Airline type: **Scheduled**

Resume required: **No**

SASE required with application: **No**

Application retained: **6 months**

Application fee: **None**

Interviews/type: **Two / group, one–on–one**

Airline pays transportation to interview: **On–line**

Height: **6' maximum**   Minimum age: **21**

Language(s) preferred: **None**

Base pay/minimum hours: **$1,225 per month/ 80
        hours**

Overtime rate: **$18/per hour**

Per diem: **$1.50/hour**

Uniform costs: **$500**

Training length/location: **21 days/PDX**

Training cost: **None**

Salary during training: **Per diem**

Company–paid housing provided: **Out–of–town
        trainees only**

Domiciles: **PDX BOI SEA GEG**

Flight attendant union: **Association of Flight
        Attendants**

Horizon Air

Attn: Personnel Department

8070 NE Airtrans Way

Portland, OR 97218–1264

Website: www.horizonair.com

✈ JETBLUE AIRWAYS

Airline type: **Scheduled**

Resume required: **Yes**

SASE required with application: **No**

Application retained: **6 months**

Application fee: **None**

Interviews/type: **Three / telephone, one–on–one, group**

Airline pays transportation to interview: **On–line**

Height: **5'1" minimum**   Minimum age: **20**

Language(s) preferred: **Second language a plus**

Base pay/minimum hours: **$20 per hour / 70 hours**

Overtime rate: **$30/hour**

Per diem: **$1.80/hour**

Uniform costs: **None**

Training length/location: **24 days / MIA JFK**

Training cost: **None**

Salary during training: **Salary pro–rated**

Company–paid housing provided: **Yes**

Domiciles: **JFK**

Flight attendant union: **None**

jetBlue Airways
Attn: In–Flight
8002 Kew Gardens Road, 6th Floor
Kew Gardens, NY 11415–3600

Instructions: Apply online.

Website: http://www.jetblue.com/

✈ LAKER BAHAMAS

Airline type: **Scheduled**

Resume required: **Yes**

SASE required with application: **No**

Application retained: **6 months**

Application fee: **None**

Interviews/type: **Two / group, private**

Airline pays transportation to interview: **On–line**

Height: **5'2 to 6'**   Minimum age: **21**

Language(s) preferred: **None**

Base pay/minimum hours: **$15 per hour / 67 hours**

Overtime rate: **None**

Per diem: **None**

Uniform costs: **$450**

Training length/location: **3 weeks / FLL**

Training cost: **None**

Salary during training: **None**

Company–paid housing provided: **Yes**

Domiciles: **FLL FPO**

Flight attendant union: **None**

Laker Bahamas
Attn: In–Flight, Suite 115
1100 Lee Wagener Blvd.
Ft. Lauderdale, FL 33315–3566

✈ MESA AIRLINES

Airline type: **Scheduled**

Resume required: **Yes**

SASE required with application: **No**

Application retained: **6 months**

Application fee: **None**

Interviews/type: **Two / individual, small group. Occasional open houses**

Airline pays transportation to interview: **On–line**

Height: **5'10" maximum**   Minimum age: **19**

Language(s) preferred: **None**

Base pay/minimum hours: **$~~13.55~~ per hour / 65 hours**   15.21

Overtime rate: **None**

Per diem: **$1/hour for overnight**

Uniform costs: **$300**

Training length/location: **4 to 6 weeks / PHX**

Training cost: **None**

Salary during training: **$100/week**

Company–paid housing provided: **Yes**

Domiciles: **CLT CMH PHL PHX GJT ~~DCA~~** , IAD, BNA

Flight attendant union: **Association of Flight Attendants**

Mesa Airlines
410 N. 44th Street
Suite 700
Phoenix, AZ 85005–7690

Instructions: Email resume to Inflight@Mesa–Air.com

Website: www.mesa–air.com

✈ MESABA AIRLINES

Airline type: **Scheduled**
Resume required: **Yes**
SASE required with application: **No**
Application retained: **6 months**
Application fee: **None**
Interviews/type: **Two / open house, one–on–one**
Airline pays transportation to interview: **On–line**
Height: **6' maximum**   Minimum age: **18**
Language(s) preferred: **None**
Base pay/minimum hours: **$15.50 per hour / 75 hours**
Overtime rate: **$15.50/hour**
Per diem: **$1.35/hour**
Uniform costs: **$530**
Training length/location: **4 weeks / MSP**
Training cost: **None**
Salary during training: **Monthly guarantee**
Company–paid housing provided: **Out–of–town trainees only**
Domiciles: **MSP DTW CWA RHI MEM CVG**
Flight attendant union: **Association of Flight Attendants**

Mesaba Airlines
Attn: In–Flight Recruiting
7501 26th Avenue South
Minneapolis, MN 55450–1021
800/777–6013

Instructions: Apply only at open house.

Website: www.mesaba.com

✈ MIAMI AIR

Airline type: **Charter**

Resume required: **Yes**

SASE required with application: **No**

Application retained: **6 months**

Application fee: **None**

Interviews/type: **Three / group, second, final**

Airline pays transportation to interview: **No**

Height: **5'1" minimum**   Minimum age: **20**

Language(s) preferred: **Spanish, French, German, Portuguese, Italian**

Base pay/minimum hours: **$16.30 per hour / 65 hours**

Overtime rate: **$16.30/hour**

Per diem: **$1.50/hour**

Uniform costs: **$500**

Training length/location: **4 weeks / MIA**

Training cost: **None**

Salary during training: **$100/week**

Company–paid housing provided: **No**

Domiciles: **MIA**

Flight attendant union: **None**

Miami Air
P.O. Box 660880
Miami Springs, FL 33266–0880
Website: www.miamiair.com

✈ MIDWAY AIRLINES

Airline type: **Scheduled**

Resume required: **Yes**

SASE required with application: **No**

Application retained: **1 month**

Application fee: **None**

Interviews/type: **Varies / group, one–on–one**

Airline pays transportation to interview: **No**

Height: **5'10½" maximum**   Minimum age: **21**

Language(s) preferred: **None**

Base pay/minimum hours: **$15 per hour / 57½ hours**

Overtime rate: **$15/hour**

Per diem: **$30/day**

Uniform costs: **$350**

Training length/location: **4 weeks / RDU**

Training cost: **None**

Salary during training: **$30/day**

Company–paid housing provided: **Yes**

Domiciles: **RDU**

Flight attendant union: **Association of Flight Attendants**

Midway Airlines

Attn: Human Resources

2801 Slater Road, Suite 200

Morrisville, NC 27560–8477

Instructions: Visit the website for upcoming hiring information.

Website: www.midwayair.com

✈ MIDWEST AIRLINES

Airline type: **Scheduled**

Resume required: **No**

SASE required with application: **No**

Application retained: **6 months**

Application fee: **None**

Interviews/type: **Two / information session and team interview, final Interview**

Airline pays transportation to interview: **On–line**

Height: **None**   Minimum age: **18**

Language(s) preferred: **Spanish, others**

Base pay/minimum hours: **$1,429 per month full–time, $715 per month part–time**

Overtime rate: **None**

Per diem: **$1/hour, $1.50/hour for overnight**

Uniform costs: **$500**

Training length/location: **6 weeks / MKE**

Training cost: **None**

Salary during training: **$8.24/hour**

Company–paid housing provided: **None**

Domiciles: **MKE**

Flight attendant union: **Association of Flight Attendants**

Midwest Airlines

Attn: Human Resources

6744 S. Howell Avenue HQ–22–A

Oak Creek, WI 53154–1402

Website: www.midwestexpress.com

✈ NATIONAL AIRLINES

Airline type: **Scheduled**

Resume required: **No**

SASE required with application: **No**

Application retained: **6 months**

Application fee: **None**

Interviews/type: **Three / group, panel, one–on–one**

Airline pays transportation to interview: **No**

Height: **None**   Minimum age: **20**

Language(s) preferred: **None**

Base pay/minimum hours: **$15,000 per year / 80 hours**

Overtime rate: **Time–and–a–half**

Per diem: **$30 to $45 per overnight**

Uniform costs: **None**

Training length/location: **4 weeks / LAS**

Training cost: **None**

Salary during training: **$140/week**

Company–paid housing provided: **No**

Domiciles: **LAS**

Flight attendant union: **None**

National Airlines
6020 Spencer Street
Las Vegas, NV 89119–2934
Fax: 702/944–2947

Instructions: Applicant must attend Job Fair.

Website: www.nationalairlines.com

✈ NORTH AMERICAN AIRLINES

Airline type: **Charter**

Resume required: **No**

SASE required with application: **No**

Application retained: **6 months**

Application fee: **None**

Interviews/type: **Two / group, private**

Airline pays transportation to interview: **No**

Height: **5'1" to 6'**   Minimum age: **20**

Language(s) preferred: **Hebrew, Spanish, French**

Base pay/minimum hours: **$19.47 per hour / 67 hours**

Overtime rate: **$29.21/hour**

Per diem: **$1.60/hour domestic, $2/hour international**

Uniform costs: **$900**

Training length/location: **4 weeks / JFK**

Training cost: **None**

Salary during training: **$25/day**

Company–paid housing provided: **No**

Domiciles: **JFK NSY BOS LFB**

Flight attendant union: **None**

North American Airlines
JFK International Airport, Bldg. 75
North Hanger Road
Jamaica, NY 11430–1817
Fax: 718/656–2536

Website: www.northamair.com

✈ NORTH–SOUTH AIRWAYS

Airline type: **Charter**
Resume required: **Yes**
SASE required with application: **No**
Application retained: **6 months**
Application fee: **None**
Interviews/type: **One / individual**
Airline pays transportation to interview: **Sometimes**
Height: **None**   Minimum age: **21**
Language(s) preferred: **None**
Base pay/minimum hours: **$24,000 per year / 75 hours**
Overtime rate: **$33.33/hour**
Per diem: **$30/day**
Uniform costs: **$50**
Training length/location: **3 weeks / ATW**
Training cost: **None**
Salary during training: **None**
Company–paid housing provided: **Yes**
Domiciles: **ATW**
Flight attendant union: **None**

North–South Airways
1954 Airport Road
Suite 200
Atlanta, GA 30341–4953
Website: www.nsair.com

✈ NORTHERN AIRLINES

Airline type: **Scheduled**

Resume required: **No**

SASE required with application: **Yes**

Application retained: **6 months**

Application fee: **None**

Interviews/type: **Three / group, panel, one–on–one**

Airline pays transportation to interview: **No**

Height: **None**   Minimum age: **21**

Language(s) preferred: **French, Spanish**

Base pay/minimum hours: **$12,500 per year / 70 hours**

Overtime rate: **$14/hour**

Per diem: **$25 per overnight**

Uniform costs: **$390**

Training length/location: **3 weeks / SYR**

Training cost: **None**

Salary during training: **$250/week**

Company–paid housing provided: **Yes**

Domiciles: **SYR**

Flight attendant union: **None**

Northern Airlines
P.O. Box 3940
Syracuse, NY 13220–3940

✈ NORTHWEST AIRLINES

Airline type: **Scheduled**

Resume required: **No**

SASE required with application: **No**

Application retained: **6 months**

Application fee: **None**

Interviews/type: **Three / phone, open house, one–on–one**

Airline pays transportation to interview: **Yes**

Height: **5'2" minimum**   Minimum age: **18**

Language(s) preferred: **None**

Base pay/minimum hours: **$1,275.78 per month / 65 hours**

Overtime rate: **$21.77/hour**

Per diem: **$1.85/hour domestic, $2.05/hour international**

Uniform costs: **$800 to $1,000**

Training length/location: **5 weeks / MSP**

Training cost: **None**

Salary during training: **$15/day**

Company–paid housing provided: **Yes**

Domiciles: **MSP DTW HNL MEM SFO LAX SEA BOS NYC**

Flight attendant union: **International Brotherhood of Teamsters**

Northwest Airlines
5101 Northwest Drive
Mail Stop F1470
St. Paul Airport, MN 55111–3034
Website: www.nwa.com

✈ OMNI AIR INTERNATIONAL

Airline type: **Charter**

Resume required: **No**

SASE required with application: **No**

Application retained: **6 months**

Application fee: **None**

Interviews/type: **Three / open house, group, group**

Airline pays transportation to interview: **No**

Height: **5'4" minimum**   Minimum age: **21**

Language(s) preferred: **None**

Base pay/minimum hours: **$17 per hour / 65 hours**

Overtime rate: **$17/hour**

Per diem: **$1.25/hour domestic, $2/hour
                international**

Uniform costs: **$600**

Training length/location: **4 weeks / Varies**

Training cost: **None**

Salary during training: **None**

Company–paid housing provided: **Out–of–town
                trainees only**

Domiciles: **LAS MSP**

Flight attendant union: **None**

Omni Air International
P.O. Box 582527
Tulsa, OK 74158–2527
918/831–3099

Instructions: Walk–ins possible. Must be able to lift 50 pounds.

Website: www.omniairintl.com

✈ PACE AIRLINES

Airline type: **Charter**

Resume required: **Yes**

SASE required with application: **No**

Application retained: **6 months**

Application fee: **None**

Interviews/type: **Two / open house, individual**

Airline pays transportation to interview: **No**

Height: **5'2" minimum** Minimum age: **19**

Language(s) preferred: **None**

Base pay/minimum hours: **Varies by domicile**

Overtime rate: **Varies by domicile**

Per diem: **Varies by domicile**

Uniform costs: **$375**

Training length/location: **3 weeks / INT**

Training cost: **None**

Salary during training: **Per diem**

Company–paid housing provided: **Yes**

Domiciles: **JFK ATW CLT IAD SDF CVG BNA MSB DAL ABE INT SFB**

Flight attendant union: **None**

Pace Airlines
Attn: Elaine Brock
P.O. Box 525
Winston–Salem, NC 27102–0525
Fax: 336/776–2266

Instructions: No phone calls please. Fax resume only.

Website: www.paceairline.com

✈ PENINSULA AIR

Airline type: **Both**

Resume required: **No**

SASE required with application: **No**

Application retained: **3 months**

Application fee: **None**

Interviews/type: **Private**

Airline pays transportation to interview: **No**

Height: **5'10" maximum**   Minimum age: **18**

Language(s) preferred: **Filipino, Japanese**

Base pay/minimum hours: **$1,900 per month**

Overtime rate: **None**

Per diem: **$35 per overnight**

Uniform costs: **$300**

Training length/location: **2 weeks / ANC**

Training cost: **None**

Salary during training: **None**

Company–paid housing provided: **None**

Domiciles: **ANC**

Flight attendant union: **None**

Peninsula Air

Attn: Human Resources

6100 Boeing Avenue

Anchorage, AK 99502–1000

Fax: 907/243–6848

Website: www.penair.com

✈ PIEDMONT AIRLINES

Airline type: **Scheduled**

Resume required: **Yes**

SASE required with application: **Yes**

Application retained: **6 months**

Application fee: **None**

Interviews/type: **Three / group, individual, individual**

Airline pays transportation to interview: **On–line only**

Height: **5'2" minimum**   Minimum age: **21**

Language(s) preferred: **Spanish**

Base pay/minimum hours: **$16.29 per hour / 72 hours**

Overtime rate: **$16.29/hour**

Per diem: **$1.30/hour**

Uniform costs: **$500 to $600**

Training length/location: **2½ weeks / SBY**

Training cost: **None**

Salary during training: **Monthly guarantee pro–rated daily**

Company–paid housing provided: **Yes**

Domiciles: **SBY TPA ROA CHO ORF/PHF EWN JAX**

Flight attendant union: **Association of Flight Attendants**

Piedmont Airlines
5443 Airport Terminal Road
Sallsbury/Wicomico Airport
Sallsbury, MD 21804–1545
Website: www.piedmont–airlines.com

✈ PINNACLE AIRLINES

Airline type: **Scheduled**

Resume required: **Yes**

SASE required with application: **No**

Application retained: **6 months**

Application fee: **None**

Interviews/type: **Three / Open house, panel, private**

Airline pays transportation to interview: **On–line**

Height: **5'1" to 5'10"**   Minimum age: **19**

Language(s) preferred: **None**

Base pay/minimum hours: **$14.44 per hour / 75 hours**

Overtime rate: **None**

Per diem: **$1.15/day**

Uniform costs: **$400**

Training length/location: **2½ weeks / MEM**

Training cost: **None**

Salary during training: **$15/day**

Company–paid housing provided: **Out–of–town trainees only**

Domiciles: **MEM MSP DTW**

Flight attendant union: **Paper and Allied Chemical Engineers**

Pinnacle Airlines
1689 Nonconnah Blvd.
Memphis, TN 38132–2102
866/924–7546

Instructions: Fax: 901/348–4162

Website: www.nwairlink.com

✈ PLANET AIRWAYS

Airline type: **Charter**
Resume required: **Yes**
SASE required with application: **No**
Application retained: **6 months**
Application fee: **None**
Interviews/type: **Three / open house, panel, individual**
Airline pays transportation to interview: **No**
Height: **None**   Minimum age: **21**
Language(s) preferred: **None**
Base pay/minimum hours: **$20 per hour / 60 hours**
Overtime rate: **Time–and–a–quarter**
Per diem: **$1.35/hour, $30 per day maximum**
Uniform costs: **$450**
Training length/location: **4 weeks / FLL**
Training cost: **None**
Salary during training: **$100/week**
Company–paid housing provided: **No**
Domiciles: **FLL**
Flight attendant union: **None**

Planet Airways
1050 Lee Wagener Blvd.
Suite 303
Ft. Lauderdale, FL 33315–3500

✈ PSA AIRLINES

Airline type: **Scheduled**

Resume required: **Yes**

SASE required with application: **No**

Application retained: **6 months**

Application fee: **None**

Interviews/type: **Two / group, individual**

Airline pays transportation to interview: **Online**

Height: **5'7" maximum**   Minimum age: **19**

Language(s) preferred: **French**

Base pay/minimum hours: **$14.33 per hour / 72 hours**

Overtime rate: **$14.33/hour**

Per diem: **$1.30/hour**

Uniform costs: **$500 to $1,000**

Training length/location: **3 weeks / DAY**

Training cost: **None**

Salary during training: **$420/week**

Company–paid housing provided: **Yes**

Domiciles: **DAY CAK TYS PIT CVG**

Flight attendant union: **Association of Flight Attendants**

PSA Airlines
3400 Terminal Drive
Vandalia, OH 45377–1041
Website: www.usairways.com

✈ RYAN INTERNATIONAL

Airline type: **Charter**

Resume required: **No**

SASE required with application: **No**

Application retained: **12 months**

Application fee: **None**

Interviews/type: **Two / group, individual**

Airline pays transportation to interview: **No**

Height: **None**   Minimum age: **21**

Language(s) preferred: **None**

Base pay/minimum hours: **$19 per hour**

Overtime rate: **None**

Per diem: **$30/overnight domestic, $35/overnight international**

Uniform costs: **None**

Training length/location: **3 weeks / Varies**

Training cost: **None**

Salary during training: **Salary pro–rated**

Company–paid housing provided: **Out–of–town trainees only**

Domiciles: **ACY BAL ORD SFO plus seasonal CLE DTW MKE MSP JFK**

Flight attendant union: **None**

Ryan International Airlines
266 North Main
Wichita, KS 67202–1504
877/269 7926

Instructions: Apply via website.

Website: www.flyryan.com

✈ SHUTTLE AMERICA

Airline type: **Scheduled**

Resume required: **Yes**

SASE required with application: **No**

Application retained: **6 months**

Application fee: **None**

Interviews/type: **Two / individual, individual**

Airline pays transportation to interview: **On–line**

Height: **None**   Minimum age: **19**

Language(s) preferred: **None**

Base pay/minimum hours: **$18 per hour / 72 hours**

Overtime rate: **$18/hour**

Per diem: **$1.35/hour**

Uniform costs: **Cost shared by company**

Training length/location: **2 weeks / BDL**

Training cost: **None**

Salary during training: **Monthly guarantee**

Company–paid housing provided: **$20/day for out–of–town trainees only**

Domiciles: **BUF BED TTN**

Flight attendant union: **None**

Shuttle America
P.O. Box 9310
Ft. Wayne, IN 46899–9310
Fax: 860/386–4243

Instructions: Apply via website.

Website: www.shuttleamerica.com

✈ SKYWAYS AIRLINES

Airline type: **Scheduled**
Resume required: **Yes**
SASE required with application: **No**
Application retained: **6 months**
Application fee: **None**
Interviews/type: **Two / private, private**
Airline pays transportation to interview: **Yes**
Height: **Proportional**   Minimum age: **19**
Language(s) preferred: **None**
Base pay/minimum hours: **$14.25 per hour / 80 hours**
Overtime rate: **None**
Per diem: **$1.10/per hour**
Uniform costs: **$400**
Training length/location: **4 weeks / MKE**
Training cost: **None**
Salary during training: **$997.50**
Company–paid housing provided: **No**
Domiciles: **MKE**
Flight attendant union: **None**

Skyways Airlines
1190 W. Rawson Avenue
Oak Creek, WI 53154–1447
414/570–2300

Instructions: Apply via website.

Website: www.midwest–express.com

✈ SKYWEST AIRLINES

Airline type: **Scheduled**
Resume required: **No**
SASE required with application: **No**
Application retained: **3 months**
Application fee: **None**
Interviews/type: **Two / group, individual**
Airline pays transportation to interview: **No**
Height: **5' to 5'8"**   Minimum age: **19**
Language(s) preferred: **None**
Base pay/minimum hours: **$17.50 per hour / 75
        hours**
Overtime rate: **$17.50/hour**
Per diem: **$1.60/hour**
Uniform costs: **$400**
Training length/location: **24 days / SLC**
Training cost: **None**
Salary during training: **$1,078**
Company–paid housing provided: **Yes**
Domiciles: **PSP FAT SBP PDX SBA DEN SMF SLC
        SAN MRY**
Flight attendant union: **None**

Skywest Airlines
444 S. River Road
St. George, UT 84790–2085
Website: www.skywest.com

✈ SOUTHEAST AIRLINES

Airline type: **Both**
Resume required: **Yes**
SASE required with application: **No**
Application retained: **12 months**
Application fee: **None**
Interviews/type: **Group**
Airline pays transportation to interview: **No**
Height: **None**   Minimum age: **20**
Language(s) preferred: **None**
Base pay/minimum hours: **$17 per hour / 70 hours**
Overtime rate: **$17/hour**
Per diem: **$1.33/hour domestic, $1.65
              international**
Uniform costs: **$260**
Training length/location: **3 weeks / PIE**
Training cost: **None**
Salary during training: **Per diem**
Company–paid housing provided: **Yes**
Domiciles: **PIE ACY GPT PHL PIT CVG**
Flight attendant union: **None**

Southeast Airlines
Attn: Director of In–Flight
12552 Belcher Road
Largo, FL 33773–3014
727/530–1315

✈ SOUTHWEST AIRLINES

Airline type: **Scheduled**

Resume required: **Yes**

SASE required with application: **No**

Application retained: **12 months**

Application fee: **None**

Interviews/type: **Two / group, second**

Airline pays transportation to interview: **On–line only**

Height: **75–inch reach**   Minimum age: **20**

Language(s) preferred: **Spanish**

Base pay/minimum hours: **$14.67 per trip (243 flight miles)**

Overtime rate: **None**

Per diem: **$2/hour**

Uniform costs: **$500**

Training length/location: **4½ weeks / DAL**

Training cost: **None**

Salary during training: **None**

Company–paid housing provided: **Non–Dallas residents only**

Domiciles: **DAL OAK BWI PHX HOU MDW MCO**

Flight attendant union: **Transport Workers Union**

Southwest Airlines

P.O. Box 36611

Love Field

Dallas, TX 75235–1611

Website: www.iflyswa.com

✈ SPIRIT AIRLINES

Airline type: **Scheduled**

Resume required: **Yes, only**

SASE required with application: **No**

Application retained: **12 months**

Application fee: **None**

Interviews/type: **Three / group, one–on–one, one–on–one**

Airline pays transportation to interview: **No**

Height: **5'2" to 6'**   Minimum age: **21**

Language(s) preferred: **Spanish**

Base pay/minimum hours: **$1,200 per month / 72 hours**

Overtime rate: **$16.67/hour**

Per diem: **$1.35/hour**

Uniform costs: **$500 to $600**

Training length/location: **4 weeks / FLL**

Training cost: **None**

Salary during training: **$25/day**

Company–paid housing provided: **None**

Domiciles: **DTW ACY FLL**

Flight attendant union: **None**

Spirit Airlines

Attn: In–Flight Recruiting

2800 Executive Way

Miramar, FL 33025–6542

954/447–8002

Website: www.spiritair.com

✈ SUN COUNTRY AIRLINES

Airline type: **Charter**

Resume required: **Yes, only**

SASE required with application: **No**

Application retained: **12 months**

Application fee: **None**

Interviews/type: **Two / group, panel**

Airline pays transportation to interview: **No**

Height: **5'1" minimum**   Minimum age: **19**

Language(s) preferred: **None**

Base pay/minimum hours: **$16.25 per hour / 70 hours**

Overtime rate: **$2/hour over 85 hours**

Per diem: **$1.25/hour domestic; $1.30/hour Canada, Mexico, Central America; $2.50/hour international**

Uniform costs: **$550**

Training length/location: **4 weeks / MSP**

Training cost: **None**

Salary during training: **$40/day**

Company–paid housing provided: **No**

Domiciles: **MSP**

Flight attendant union: **International Brotherhood of Teamsters**

Sun Country Airlines
1300 Mendota Heights Road
Mendota Heights, MN 55120–1128

Instructions: See website for additional information.

Website: www.suncountry.com

✈ SUNWORLD

Airline type: **Scheduled**

Resume required: **Yes**

SASE required with application: **No**

Application retained: **6 months**

Application fee: **None**

Interviews/type: **Two / group, one–on–one**

Airline pays transportation to interview: **No**

Height: **5'2" minimum**   Minimum age: **21**

Language(s) preferred: **Second language a plus**

Base pay/minimum hours: **$18,000 per year / 80 hours**

Overtime rate: **Time–and–a–half**

Per diem: **$30/overnight**

Uniform costs: **$350**

Training length/location: **3 weeks / CVG**

Training cost: **None**

Salary during training: **Allowance**

Company–paid housing provided: **Yes**

Domiciles: **CVG IND PHL**

Flight attendant union: **None**

Sunworld

P.O. Box 75030

Cincinnati, OH 45275–0003

859/767–7181

Website: www.sunworld–air.com

✈ TRANS MERIDIAN

Airline type: **Charter**

Resume required: **Yes**

SASE required with application: **No**

Application retained: **6 months**

Application fee: **None**

Interviews/type: **Two / group, secondary**

Airline pays transportation to interview: **No**

Height: **None**   Minimum age: **18**

Language(s) preferred: **Spanish**

Base pay/minimum hours: **$18 per hour / 60 hours**

Overtime rate: **$18/hour**

Per diem: **$1.50/hour**

Uniform costs: **$470**

Training length/location: **2½ weeks / Usually at hiring city**

Training cost: **None**

Salary during training: **None**

Company–paid housing provided: **No**

Domiciles: **MSP BOS**

Flight attendant union: **None**

Trans Meridian
680 Thornton Way
Lithia Springs, GA 30122–2600
770/732–6900

Website: www.transmeridian–airlines.com

✈ TRANS STATES AIRLINES

Airline type: **Scheduled**

Resume required: **Yes**

SASE required with application: **Yes**

Application retained: **6 months**

Application fee: **None**

Interviews/type: **Two / group, panel**

Airline pays transportation to interview: **No**

Height: **5'1" to 5'7"**   Minimum age: **19**

Language(s) preferred: **Second language preferred**

Base pay/minimum hours: **$13.75 per hour (STL),
                    $14.75 per hour (RIC) / 68 hours**

Overtime rate: **None**

Per diem: **$1.05/hour**

Uniform costs: **$500**

Training length/location: **5 weeks / at base**

Training cost: **None**

Salary during training: **Base rate, retroactive**

Company–paid housing provided: **No**

Domiciles: **STL RIC**

Flight attendant union: **International Brotherhood
                    of Teamsters**

Trans States Airlines
Attn: In–Flight
4534 S. Lindbergh Blvd., Suite 302
Bridgeton, MO 63044–2243
314/895–6115

Instructions: Email resumes to:
plantee@transstates.net

Website: www.transstates.net

✈ UNITED AIRLINES

Airline type: **Scheduled**

Resume required: **No**

SASE required with application: **No**

Application retained: **12 months**

Application fee: **None**

Interviews/type: **Two / group, private**

Airline pays transportation to interview: **Yes, final only**

Height: **5'2" to 6'2"**   Minimum age: **19**

Language(s) preferred: **Cantonese, Mandarin, Japanese, French, Spanish, Korean, German, Italian, Portuguese**

Base pay/minimum hours: **$19.82 per hour / 65 hours**

Overtime rate: **$19.82/hour**

Per diem: **$1.85/hour domestic, $2.10/hour international**

Uniform costs: **$700**

Training length/location: **5½ weeks / ORD**

Training cost: **None**

Salary during training: **None**

Company–paid housing provided: **Yes**

Domiciles: **DEN JFK EWR HKG SCL FRA ~~MIA PHL~~ LAS NRT ORD DCA ~~TPE~~ LAX SFO SEA HNL LHR CDG BOS ~~LAS~~ HKG SCL**

Flight attendant union: **Association of Flight Attendants**

United Airlines

Application Request Center
EXOES P.O. Box 66100
Chicago, IL 60666–0100
Website: www.ual.com

✈ USA 300 AIRLINES

Airline type: **Both**

Resume required: **Yes**

SASE required with application: **No**

Application retained: **12 months**

Application fee: **None**

Interviews/type: **Three / group, open house, private**

Airline pays transportation to interview: **No**

Height: **None**   Minimum age: **20**

Language(s) preferred: **None**

Base pay/minimum hours: **$20,000 per year**

Overtime rate: **$200 to $400 per day**

Per diem: **$35/day for overnights**

Uniform costs: **Company paid**

Training length/location: **4 weeks / ORD, PHL, EWR**

Training cost: **None**

Salary during training: **Training allowance**

Company–paid housing provided: **None**

Domiciles: **PHL ORD EWR**

Flight attendant union: **None**

USA 3000 Airlines
335 Bishop Hollow Road
Newtown Square, PA 19073–3213
Website: www.usa3000.com

✈ USAIRWAYS

Airline type: **Scheduled**

Resume required: **No**

SASE required with application: **No**

Application retained: **6 months**

Application fee: **None**

Interviews/type: **Two / phone, one–on–one**

Airline pays transportation to interview: **On–line**

Height: **None**   Minimum age: **20**

Language(s) preferred: **French, Dutch, Italian, German, and Spanish**

Base pay/minimum hours: **$20 per hour / 71 hours**

Overtime rate: **$20/hour**

Per diem: **$1.90/hour domestic, $2.10/hour international**

Uniform costs: **$1,000**

Training length/location: **6 weeks / PIT**

Training cost: **None**

Salary during training: **None**

Company–paid housing provided: **Yes**

Domiciles: **PIT PHL DCA BWI BOS CLT**

Flight attendant union: **Association of Flight Attendants**

USAirways

2345 Crystal Drive

Arlington, VA 22227–0001

877/US–JOB–4–U

Website: **www.usairways.com**

✈ VANGUARD AIRLINES

Airline type: **Scheduled**

Resume required: **Yes**

SASE required with application: **No**

Application retained: **12 months**

Application fee: **None**

Interviews/type: **Two / group, individual**

Airline pays transportation to interview: **On–line**

Height: **5' minimum**   Minimum age: **21**

Language(s) preferred: **None**

Base pay/minimum hours: **$15.50 per hour / 75 hours**

Overtime rate: **$15.50/hour**

Per diem: **$30/day**

Uniform costs: **$350**

Training length/location: **4 weeks / MCI**

Training cost: **None**

Salary during training: **None**

Company–paid housing provided: **Yes**

Domiciles: **MCI**

Flight attendant union: **None**

Vanguard Airlines
594 Mexico City Avenue
Kansas City, MO 64153–1108
Fax: 816/243–2937

Instructions: Apply via website or email worknow@flyvanguard.com

Website: www.flyvanguard.com

✈ WORLD AIRWAYS

Airline type: **Charter**

Resume required: **Yes, only**

SASE required with application: **No**

Application retained: **6 months**

Application fee: **None**

Interviews/type: **Three / open house, panel, one–on–one**

Airline pays transportation to interview: **No**

Height: **Proportional**   Minimum age: **21**

Language(s) preferred: **Second language a plus**

Base pay/minimum hours: **$1,274.35 per month / 65 hours**

Overtime rate: **$22.55/hour**

Per diem: **$55/day**

Uniform costs: **$700**

Training length/location: **4 weeks / IAD**

Training cost: **None**

Salary during training: **Per diem**

Company–paid housing provided: **No**

Domiciles: **IAD SEA**

Flight attendant union: **International Brotherhood of Teamsters**

World Airways

HLH Building

101 World Drive

Peachtree City, GA 30269–0000

Instructions: Apply via website.

Website: www.worldair.com

Remember that a Canadian airline can hire only Canadian citizens or resident aliens wIth a current work permit. Also note that many Canadian airlines require fluency in both French and English.

Pay scales are in Canadian dollars unless specified otherwise.

Be sure to read the previous chapters before examining these airline listings.

See page 167 to learn how to receive free updates to these listings.

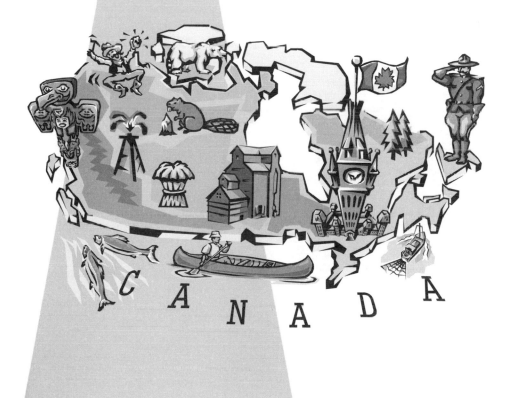

✈ AIR CANADA

Airline type: **Scheduled**

Resume required: **No**

SASE required with application: **No**

Application retained: **6 months**

Application fee: **None**

Interviews/type: **Two / individual, group**

Airline pays transportation to interview: **No**

Height: **5'2" minimum**   Minimum age: **18**

Language(s) preferred: **English, French**

Base pay/minimum hours: **$27.13 per hour / 75 hours**

Overtime rate: **None**

Per diem: **$12.87 breakfast, $14.58 lunch, $28.88 dinner, $7.54 snack**

Uniform costs: **None**

Training length/location: **7 weeks / at base**

Training cost: **None**

Salary during training: **Yes**

Company–paid housing provided: **Out–of–town trainees only**

Domiciles: **YUL YYZ YVR YYC YWG YEG**

Flight attendant union: **CUPE**

Air Canada
P.O. Box 14000
St. Laurent
Dorval, QC H4Y 1H4

Instructions: Apply only via website at http://www.aircanada.ca/about–us/employment/

Website: www.aircanada.ca

✈ AIR CREEBEC

Airline type: **Scheduled**
Resume required: **Yes**
SASE required with application: **No**
Application retained: **6 months**
Application fee: **None**
Interviews/type: **Varies**
Airline pays transportation to interview: **Possible**
Height: **None** Minimum age: **18**
Language(s) preferred: **English, French**
Base pay/minimum hours: **$21.42 per hour**
Overtime rate: **None**
Per diem: **$40/day meal allowance**
Uniform costs: **$500**
Training length/location: **5 weeks / YTS**
Training cost: **None**
Salary during training: **$10/hour**
Company–paid housing provided: **Yes**
Domiciles: **YTS YVO YUL**
Flight attendant union: **None**

Air Creebec
Timmons Airport
RR #2
Timmons, ON R4N 7C3
Website: www.aircreebec.ca

✈ AIR TRANSAT

Airline type: **Charter**

Resume required: **Yes**

SASE required with application: **No**

Application retained: **6 months**

Application fee: **None**

Interviews/type: **Four / phone, group, individual, medical**

Airline pays transportation to interview: **No**

Height: **5'2" minimum**   Minimum age: **18**

Language(s) preferred: **English, French, Italian, Portuguese, Greek, German, Dutch**

Base pay/minimum hours: **$20.25 per hour / 75 hours**

Overtime rate: **Time–and–a–half over 85 hours**

Per diem: **$3.25/hour domestic, $4/hour international**

Uniform costs: **None**

Training length/location: **5 weeks / YMX**

Training cost: **None**

Salary during training: **$7.25/hour**

Company–paid housing provided: **Out–of–town trainees only**

Domiciles: **YVR YYZ YMX**

Flight attendant union: **CUPE**

Air Transat
11600 Cargo Road A–1
Montreal International Airport
Mirabell, QC J7N 1G7

Instructions: Email resume to rh@airtransat.ca

Website: www.airtransat.ca

✈ CALM AIR INTERNATIONAL

Airline type: **Both**

Resume required: **Yes**

SASE required with application: **No**

Application retained: **6 months**

Application fee: **None**

Interviews/type: **One / panel**

Airline pays transportation to interview: **No**

Height: **None**   Minimum age: **19**

Language(s) preferred: **English, French**

Base pay/minimum hours: **$23.05 per hour / 75 hours**

Overtime rate: **Varies**

Per diem: **$47/overnight**

Uniform costs: **None**

Training length/location: **6 weeks / YWG YTH**

Training cost: **None**

Salary during training: **$6.25/hour**

Company–paid housing provided: **Out–of–town trainees only**

Domiciles: **YWG YTH**

Flight attendant union: **CUPE**

Calm Air International
90 Thompson Drive
Thompson, MB R8N 1Y8
Website: www.calmair.com

✈ CANADIAN NORTH AIRLINES

Airline type: **Scheduled**

Resume required: **Yes**

SASE required with application: **No**

Application retained: **6 months**

Application fee: **None**

Interviews/type: **Two / phone, individual**

Airline pays transportation to interview: **On–line**

Height: **None**   Minimum age: **18**

Language(s) preferred: **English/French, Inuktitut or other Northern languages**

Base pay/minimum hours: **$2,155.60 per month / 80 hours**

Overtime rate: **Time–and–a–half**

Per diem: **$8 to $10 per block hour**

Uniform costs: **None**

Training length/location: **4 weeks / YYC**

Training cost: **None**

Salary during training: **Yes**

Company–paid housing provided: **Out–of–town trainees only**

Domiciles: **YYC YEG YZF**

Flight attendant union: **Internal association**

Canadian North Airlines

5201 50th Avenue

Suite 300

Yellowknife, NT X1A 3S9

Website: www.canadiannorth.com

✈ CANJET AIRLINES

Airline type: **Scheduled**

Resume required: **Yes**

SASE required with application: **No**

Application retained: **6 months**

Application fee: **None**

Interviews/type: **Two / phone (French), one–on–one**

Airline pays transportation to interview: **No**

Height: **None**   Minimum age: **19**

Language(s) preferred: **English, French**

Base pay/minimum hours: **$18,000 per year / 75 hours**

Overtime rate: **Time–and–a–half**

Per diem: **$40/day**

Uniform costs: **Company paid**

Training length/location: **3 weeks / YHZ**

Training cost: **None**

Salary during training: **Base salary**

Company–paid housing provided: **None**

Domiciles: **YHZ**

Flight attendant union: **None**

CanJet Airlines
Attn: Rob Burns
P.O. Box 980
Halifax, NS B2T 1R6

Instructions: See website for more information.

Website: www.canjet.com

✈ FIRST AIR

Airline type: **Scheduled**
Resume required: **Yes**
SASE required with application: **No**
Application retained: **6 months**
Application fee: **None**
Interviews/type: **Three / Elimination**
Airline pays transportation to interview: **No**
Height: **None**   Minimum age: **19**
Language(s) preferred: **Inuktituk, English, French**
Base pay/minimum hours: **Varies / 65 hours**
Overtime rate: **None**
Per diem: **Varies**
Uniform costs: **None**
Training length/location: **5 weeks / YOW**
Training cost: **None**
Salary during training: **$225/week**
Company–paid housing provided: **No**
Domiciles: **YOW YZF**
Flight attendant union: **CUPE**

First Air
100 Thad Johnson Road
McDonald Cartier International Airport
Ottawa, ON K1V 0R1
Fax: 613–688–2636

Instructions: Resumes only.

Website: www.firstair.ca

✈ JAZZ / AIR CANADA REGIONAL AIRLINES

Airline type: **Scheduled**

Resume required: **Yes**

SASE required with application: **No**

Application retained: **6 months**

Application fee: **None**

Interviews/type: **Three / phone (French), group, group**

Airline pays transportation to interview: **On–line**

Height: **None**   Minimum age: **19**

Language(s) preferred: **English, French**

Base pay/minimum hours: **$26 per hour / 75 hours**

Overtime rate: **None**

Per diem: **$54/day**

Uniform costs: **$300**

Training length/location: **6 weeks / Pending**

Training cost: **None**

Salary during training: **$12,000/year**

Company–paid housing provided: **Out–of–town trainees only**

Domiciles: **YVR YYC YYZ YUL YQB YHZ YXE YYJ YXU**

Flight attendant union: **International Brotherhood of Teamsters**

Air Canada Regional Airlines
310 Goudey Drive
Halifax International Airport
Enfield, NS B2T 1E4

Instructions: Resume only. No phone calls.

Website: www.aircanadaregional.ca

✈ PROVINCIAL AIRLINES

Airline type: **Scheduled**
Resume required: **Yes**
SASE required with application: **No**
Application retained: **6 months**
Application fee: **None**
Interviews/type: **Three / HR, In–Flight, Personal**
Airline pays transportation to interview: **Online**
Height: **5'9" maximum**   Minimum age: **19**
Language(s) preferred: **French, English**
Base pay/minimum hours: **Pending**
Overtime rate: **Pending**
Per diem: **Pending**
Uniform costs: **50/50 split**
Training length/location: **4 weeks / YYT**
Training cost: **None**
Salary during training: **Pending**
Company–paid housing provided: **No**
Domiciles: **YYT**
Flight attendant union: **None**

Provincial Airlines
Human Resources Manager
P.O. Box 29030
St. Johns, NF A1A 5B5
Website: www.provair.com

✈ SKY SERVICE

Airline type: **Charter**

Resume required: **Yes**

SASE required with application: **No**

Application retained: **6 months**

Application fee: **None**

Interviews/type: **Four / one–on–one, one–on–one, group, role play**

Airline pays transportation to interview: **No**

Height: **5'3" minimum**   Minimum age: **19**

Language(s) preferred: **English, French, Spanish, Italian, Portuguese**

Base pay/minimum hours: **$19.50 per hour / 75 hours**

Overtime rate: **$19.50/hour**

Per diem: **$3.25/hour**

Uniform costs: **None**

Training length/location: **27 days / YYZ**

Training cost: **None**

Salary during training: **2½ hours/day**

Company–paid housing provided: **No**

Domiciles: **YYZ**

Flight attendant union: **None**

Sky Service
Attn: Director of In–Flight
5501 Electra Road
Mississauga, ON L5P 1B1
Website: www.skyservice.com

✈ WESTJET AIRLINES

Airline type: **Scheduled**

Resume required: **Yes**

SASE required with application: **No**

Application retained: **6 months**

Application fee: **None**

Interviews/type: **Two / group, individual**

Airline pays transportation to interview: **No**

Height: **None**   Minimum age: **18**

Language(s) preferred: **French**

Base pay/minimum hours: **$20.55 per hour / 40 hours per week**

Overtime rate: **Time–and–a–half**

Per diem: **$1.75/hour**

Uniform costs: **None**

Training length/location: **2 weeks / YYC**

Training cost: **None**

Salary during training: **$50/day**

Company–paid housing provided: **None**

Domiciles: **YYC**

Flight attendant union: **None**

WestJet Airlines
Attn: Employment
575 Palmer Road NE
Calgary, AB T2E 7G5

Instructions: Apply online via website.

Website: www.westjet.com

✈ FREE UPDATES

The information contained in the airline listings changes pretty quickly. For example, during the final production of the first edition of this book, a dozen airlines went out of business and a half dozen new ones were established. As part of your purchase price, you are entitled to an unlimited number of free updates of the airline listings in Chapter 25 until the next edition of this book is published. You should check for updates at least every four to six weeks.

Visit either of the following websites on the Internet to get the latest free "Update Sheet" for this book:

http://jobfindersonline.com

or

http://www.FlightAttendantCareerGuide.com/faupdate.cfm

Books on Flight Attendant Careers

Footsteps in the Sky

Helen McLaughlin
$24.95, 330 pages, 1994, second edition

Available from State of the Art, Ltd., 4942 Morrison Rd, Denver, CO 80219; phone: 303/936–1978, weekdays, 9 a.m. to 5 p.m. Mountain time. Add $3 for shipping.

McLaughlin presents firsthand accounts from the early stewardesses to present–day flight attendants. Loaded with photographs, this hefty tome will prepare you well for interviews for flight attendant positions. This is the book to read if you want to really understand the nature of this profession and go into your job interviews with a thorough knowledge of the history of flight attendants and the field's most famous practitioners.

Flight Attendant:
From Career Planning to Professional Service

Alice Musbach and Barbara Davis
Crown Publishers, Inc.
Out of print, but available in libraries and for purchase from Book Depot (800/438–2750) of Miami Beach, Florida, or Book Look (800/223–0540) of Warwick, New York.

"The only other career guide I recommend for flight attendant applicants." — Tim Kirkwood, author of the *Flight Attendant Job Finder & Career Guide*

From Sky Girl to Flight Attendant

Georgia Panter–Nielson
$9.00 (includes shipping), 160 pages, 1982
Air Reporter
3025 Zion Lane
San Jose, CA 95152

The story of the first stewardess union and the transformation of the occupation from a temporary job into a profession.

Resources for Finding Jobs

Airline Employee Placement Service
P.O. Box 550010
Fort Lauderdale, FL 33355
954/472–6684
Website:
http://www.aeps.com

If you are not a member, select "10 Days Free" which allows you to see sample job listings. You can also sign up for the free "Email Job Alerts" — emails sent to you on a regular basis that include job openings in the fields you select. More than 6,000 companies worldwide post jobs on the site and search the database for potential employees.

The other key feature of this site is its job database. You must join to use it. Jobs are left on the database for 90 days. About five new jobs, including flight attendant positions, are added every day.

Airline Employment Assistance Corps
P.O. Box 46251
Aurora, CO 80046
303/683–2322
Website:
http://www.aeac.net

Select "Table of Contents" to see what is on this extensive site. You will need to join ($15/month) to access the AEAC's large database of job vacancies for every type of job in aviation, including flight attendant positions. Also available here are links to more than 350 aviation–related websites and news groups.

Airline Information Service Guide
U.S. Information Services
10548 Eastborne Ave., Suite 303
Los Angeles, CA 90024

This guide ($9.95) provides contact names and addresses of where to send your resume (includes phone and fax numbers of hiring personnel) for flight attendants, pilots, ticket agent sales, baggage loaders, mechanics, ground personnel, marketing, and customer service positions.

Professional Organizations

National Business Aircraft Association
1200 Eighteenth Street NW, Suite 400
Washington, DC 20036–2506
202/783–9000
Corporate Flight Attendant Liaison: Jay Evans
(202-783-9353)
Website:
http://www.nbaa.org

General business aviation association dedicated to sharing and promoting safety, ideas, standards, and operational procedures for corporate and business aviation. There are about 50,000 members worldwide.

Women In Corporate Aviation
Contact: Elizabeth Clark, Chairperson
Website:
http://www.wca-intl.org

This group of aviation professionals including flight department personnel, FBO managers, writers, students, training center professionals, and others who network and promote career opportunities in business aviation, held its first meeting at the 1993 Women in Aviation Conference.

Women in Aviation, International
Contact: Peggy Batey Chabrian, President
Website:
http://www.wiai.org

Women in Aviation, International, is a nonprofit organization that works for the advancement of women in all aviation career fields and interests. Its 5,500 members include astronauts, corporate pilots, maintenance technicians, air traffic controllers, business owners, educators, journalists, flight attendants, high school and university students, air show performers, and airport managers.

Corporate Jet Link, Ltd.
8702 164th Avenue NE, Suite B103
Redmond, WA 98052
Toll–free: 866/JET–LINK; 425/869–7499,
cell phone: 206/915–5165, fax: 425/869–7668
Email: jstuart@corporatejetlink.com
Contact: Ms. Joni J. Stuart, President
Website:
http://corporatejetlink.com

Corporate Jet Link, Ltd. is a new interactive website that links corporate aviation professionals, including flight attendants. You can place your resume in the site's online resume bank for $10.95 per month by becoming a "member." Direct email and website access are available to members who have placed their resume online here.

Training Opportunities

Corporate Flight Attendant Training
210 Locust Street, Suite 30F
Philadelphia, PA 19106
215/625–4811, fax: 215/413–9013
Contact: Susan C. Friedenberg
Email: scffatraining@aol.com
Website:
http://www.corporateflightattendanttraining.com

Designed for the person who wants to learn about corporate aviation, this training program focuses on the necessary skills, tools, and basic standard operational procedures most corporate business aviation flight departments use. The training lasts two days, with a curriculum covering specific job–related procedures, including catering information, marketing tools, managing yourself as a business, corporate flight department interaction, international trip planning, professional image development, corporate client culture, and the A to Z's needed to be a successful corporate flight attendant. Training is conducted in Long Beach, Philadelphia, Chicago, Dallas, and London.

Flight Safety International
Gulfstream Learning Center
P.O. Box 2307
Savannah, GA 31402
800/625–9369 (toll–free)
Contacts: Beth Ganley, Lori Harvey
Website:
http:www.flightsafety.com
Offers initial and recurrent "corporate specific" emergency and first–aid training with both class-room and real–life simulation drills in a corporate cabin trainer, and in a mock–up of an aircraft and over–wing exit area over an Olympic–size pool. Excellent drills for fire fighting.

InFlight Excellence:
Executive Service & Emergency Training
P. O. Box 2421
Mission Viejo, CA 92690
949/348–1889
Contacts: Donna Casacchia, Linda Masters
Website:
www.inflightexcellence.com
InFight Excellence's initial training teaches a cockpit and cabin crew to assess an emergency situation and work as a team to resolve the problem or achieve the best possible outcome of the emergency. First–aid training is included. Recurrent training is also available

Medaire, Inc.
80 East Rio Salado Parkway, Suite 610
Tempe, AZ 85283
480/333–3700
Email: info@medaire.com
Contact: Kathleen Sieperman, vice president of education services
Website:
http://www.medaire.com
As an education resource for aviation professionals, MedAire offers a variety of instructor–led and web–based medical training courses. The company also co–authored the first *Manual of Inflight Medical Care*, an instruction manual that provides flight crews with step–by–step guidance for handling inflight medical emergencies.

Aviation Personnel International
P.O. Box 6846
New Orleans, LA 70174
504/3920-3456, fax: 504/392-3458
Contact: Janice K. Barden, industrial psychologist
Email: avperint@bellsouth.net

API is an aviation industry placement service for all positions within corporate aviation.

Survival Systems Training USA
144 Tower Avenue
Groton, CT 06340
888/386-5371 (toll-free), 860/405-0002, fax: 860/405-0006
Contact: Richard E. McInnis, Vice President
Website:
http:www.survivalsystemsinc.com

Survival Systems instructs pilots, aircrew, and passengers in water aircraft ditching emergency and escape procedures, as well as rescue and sea survival techniques. Survival Systems also provides U.S. Coast Guard–approved open–water sea survival training under all climatic conditions for both aviation and marine interests. Located at the Groton–New London Airport in Groton, CT, its sophisticated training center features a 100,000–gallon (30 feet wide by 40 feet long by 14 feet deep) training tank and the world's most advanced aircraft–ditching simulator, the Modular Egress Training Simulator (METS™). The METS™ demonstrates real–time aircraft immersion and inversion, and features exit–specific technology that replicates more than a dozen types of fixed–wing and rotary aircraft.

FACTS® Training International / AirCare International, Ltd.
3633 81st Avenue SW
Olympia, WA 98512-7461
800/754-9805 (toll-free), fax: 360/754-1911
Contact: Dorene Mykol
Website:
http://www.aircare.com

A systematic human factors approach to crew member emergency and first–aid training geared for corporate aviation. Offers hands–on drills and practice on cabin emergency simulators providing a realistic experience

Corporate Flight Attendants
1100 New Highway, Suite 14
Republic Airport
Farmingdale, New York 11735
631/391–9228, fax: 631/845–7221
Contacts: Kathy Jones, Debra McGown

A contract flight attendant placement agency committed to excellence and "corporate specific" safety trained personnel, CFA serves New Jersey, New York, Connecticut, and Pennsylvania.

InFlight Management Services
New York City, New York
212/687–2558
Contact person: Shirlaine Hayes

InFlight is a contract flight attendant agency.

Aviation International News
214 Franklin Avenue
Midland Park, NJ 07432
201/444–5075, fax: 201/444.4647
Website:
http://www.ainonline.com

An extremely informative magazine about business, commercial, and regional aviation.

Erica Sheward's Training Program:
Food Safety, Security, Food Borne Pathogens, Passenger Health & You

Castle Kitchens Executive Catering

Castle Farm Estate

The Hollow
Washington, West Sussex RH20 3DA
United Kingdom
Telephone (from the USA) 011-44-1903-891400
Fax (from the USA) 011-44-1903-891414
Contact: Erica Sheward
Website:
http://www.castle–kitchens.com

This program teaches flight attendants how to implement global food safety hazard legislation on the job. The introduction of HACCP (Hazard Analysis

Critical Control Point) into the flight attendant training ethic has been revolutionary. A long–standing practice and procedure in the food production and service industry, HACCP is a simply documented system designed and modified for flight attendants that encourages a heightened awareness of the hazards involved in every practice connected with the ordering, storing, and handling food for the cabin.

Related Book Resources

The following resources are available from Planning/ Communications, 7215 Oak Ave., River Forest, IL 60305. Order by mail or toll–free, 888/366–5200 weekdays, 9 a.m. to 6 p.m. Central time. Add $6/ shipping for the first item plus $1 for each additional item.

Also available online at http://jobfindersonline.com

International Job Finder: Where the Jobs are Worldwide
Daniel Lauber with Kraig Rice
$19.95/paperback, $32.95/hard cover
2002, 348 pages, Add $6/shipping.

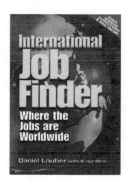

"**Terrific** book... truly **indispensable** for international job seekers." — *Joyce Lain Kennedy, nationally–syndicated career columnist*

If your goal is to live and work abroad, now is the time to spread your wings. Finding the fabulous international jobs and careers across the globe used to difficult, but today the Internet bridges the gaps of time and distance to bring hundreds of thousands of international job opportunities to your desktop. The *International Job Finder* guides you past the hype to provide details on over 1,200 online and print sources of job openings, salary surveys, and directories of companies the worldwide.

"...a straightforward presentation with all the facts and all the dirt on jobs involving living and working abroad. Of special merit is the advice for avoiding international job scams, adapting to the host nation's culture, and safeguarding against anti–American threats.... an essential and invaluable resource... for anyone serious about job–hunting abroad." — *Midwest Book Review*

How to Get a Job with a Cruise Line, 5th ed.
Mary Fallon Miller
$16.95, 2001, 336 pages, fifth edition

 You'll never fall victim to one of those employment scams offering unspecified jobs with cruise lines if you get this book. This in–depth, all–new edition provides everything you need to know about the 180 different jobs available with cruise lines, job application tips from personnel directors, and the most complete directory of cruise lines and concessionaires throughout the world. For each of the 40 cruise lines, you get the scoop on its history, highlights, classification, where they cruise and in which seasons, details on each ship in its fleet, newly built ships, nationality of crew and staff, profile of guests, job hotline and website, background requirements, and the full address for submitting your job application. Learn about the ten best ways to apply for cruise line jobs, opportunities for youth counselors at sea, and travel and tourism training programs.

✈ SIGN UP YOUR FRIENDS

Many of your friends may be interested in becoming flight attendants for today's airlines. Sign them up for their own copy of *The Flight Attendant Job Finder and Career Guide*. After all, it's much more fun to work with friends!

To obtain another copy:

Visit your local bookstore

or

Order with a credit card on the Internet
from our secure site at:

http://jobfindersonline.com

or

Call the publisher, Planning/Communications,
toll–free, weekdays between
9 a.m. and 6 p.m. Central Standard Time at:

888/366–5200

or

Send your check or money order payable to:

Planning/Communications

Dept. FAJF77
7215 Oak Avenue
River Forest, IL 60305–1935

Be sure to include $5.50 for shipping within the U.S. ($7.50/Canada, $16/elsewhere) in addition to the $16.95 price of the book.
Illinois residents should add 7.75% sales tax.

To contact the author, send an email
to Tim Kirkwood at:

tim@planningcommunications.com

or

visit Tim's website at:
http://www.FlightAttendantCareerGuide.com

Born in 1953 in Bloomington, Minnesota, Tim Kirkwood began his travel career with a sales position that led him to the southeastern United States and eventually to California. He began his flight attendant career in San Francisco when TWA hired him in 1976. He has been based in Kansas City, Boston, and New York City. He has survived deregulation, labor disputes, industry cutbacks, and corporate takeovers.

The flexible scheduling of his flight attendant career has allowed Tim to pursue many other vocations, including disk jockey, tour director, bartender, and author.

The frequent use of his flight attendant travel benefits has given him the opportunity to excel as a professional photographer in both standard and stereo (3–D) formats. Tim has also been involved in many volunteer activities for charity.

Tim frequently conducts seminars on how to become a flight attendant. He is also the "Flight Attendant Representative" for the **Aviation Employee Placement Service** — an Internet–based job placement service for jobs in all aspects of aviation located on the Internet at: http://www.aeps.com

Tim currently lives in south Florida.